Edmonton's
Urban Villages

The Community League Movement

Ron Kuban

Edmonton's
Urban Villages

The Community League Movement

THE UNIVERSITY OF ALBERTA PRESS

Published by

The University of Alberta Press
Ring House 2
Edmonton, Alberta T6G 2E1

Copyright © Ron Kuban 2005
ISBN 0–88864–438–8

Library and Archives Canada Cataloguing in Publication

Kuban, Ron, 1953—
    Edmonton's urban villages : the community league movement / Ron Kuban.

    Includes bibliographical references and index.
    ISBN 0–88864–438–8

    1. Edmonton Federation of Community Leagues–History. 2. Community organization–
Alberta–Edmonton–History. 3. Citizens' associations–Alberta–Edmonton–History.
4. Edmonton (Alta.)–History. 5. Municipal government–Alberta–Edmonton–Citizen
participation–History. 6. City planning–Alberta–Edmonton–Citizen participation–History.
7. Voluntarism–Alberta–Edmonton--History. I. Title.

FC3696.394.K82 2005	971.23'34	C2005–902861–0

The University of Alberta Press is committed to protecting our natural environment. As part of our
efforts, this book is printed on Enviro Paper: it contains 100% post-consumer recycled fibres and is
acid- and chlorine-free.

The University of Alberta Press gratefully acknowledges the support received for its publishing
program from The Canada Council for the Arts. The University of Alberta Press also gratefully
acknowledges the financial support of the Government of Canada through the Book Publishing
Industry Development Program (BPIDP) and from the Alberta Foundation for the Arts for its
publishing activities.

Canada Council Conseil des Arts
for the Arts du Canada

Dedicated to volunteers (past, present, and future),
to my wife Wendy,
and to our two children, Kaitlyn and Mitchell,
who embody the volunteer spirit.

Contents

Acknowledgements

Writing a book is an adventure. To begin with, it is a toy, then an amusement. Then it becomes a mistress, and then it becomes a monster, then it becomes a tyrant. And, the last phase is that just as you are about to become reconciled to your servitude, you kill the monster and reel him about to the public.

– SIR WINSTON CHURCHILL

THE ACHIEVEMENT OF ANY VENTURE worthy of boasting rights is never reached single-handedly. Much like the story told across its pages, this book is a reflection of the effort of countless dedicated and talented individuals, each contributing a piece that has made the tapestry of our community a thing of beauty. Mark Twain noted, "Great people are those who make others feel that they too can become great." This book tells the story of many such "great people"— coaches, community planners, social activists, and caring neighbours—who along the last eighty-seven-plus years have toiled to make their neighbourhood a community, and thereby raise the quality of life for all its residents. Regrettably, only a relative few of these folks are mentioned by name, with countless others—each an incredible person in his or her own right—being discussed as a group, and part of a movement. Henry David Thoreau stated, "The hero is commonly the simplest and obscurest of men." Truth be told, the countless community volunteers who are not mentioned here are the unrewarded heroes, the essence of this story, and in need of difficult-to-give acknowledgement.

The writing of this story was a labour of love, greatly aided by a number of organizations and individuals. My thanks to the Edmonton Federation of Community Leagues (EFCL) board and staff, who provided me much support and encouragement. A number of EFCL personnel are worthy of special mention. One such person—Bernice Neufeld—is a fierce protector of Edmonton's community league movement and has served it in many capacities, most recently (until April 2004) as the EFCL executive director. I am particularly grateful to Bernice for sharing her wealth of knowledge and her research ability. She guided me well during my three-year term as EFCL president and served as a tremendous resource in the writing of this book by reminding me of important events, persons, and issues.

Edo Nyland is another phenomenal volunteer-activist on behalf of community leagues. He is currently the EFCL board member in charge of special projects, which involves EFCL activities relating to Edmonton and Alberta centenary celebrations. During 2004, these included a renewal of the Soap Box Derby, a presentation of A Memory Box (a play about the EFCL history), and this book project. I am grateful to Edo for his support, encouragement, and editing efforts.

Three other key EFCL representatives are also worthy of mention for their assistance and encouragement. They are Don Kuchelyma, Shane Berghahl, and Russ Dahms, who are respectively the EFCL recent past president, current president, and executive director. To them, plus the board and staff of the EFCL my sincere thanks.

My thanks are extended to the EFCL's long-standing partner, the City of Edmonton, and in particular to the Edmonton City Archives, which donated from its collection many of the photographs in this book. The City Archives staff members, especially Glynys Hohmann, have been particularly helpful in identifying or finding appropriate pictures.

I am also deeply indebted to a number of individuals who took time from their busy lives to comment on the book's content and direction. Their feedback improved my work and made it more pleasant to read. I hereby offer my thanks to Arlene Meldrum for her insight into the EFCL, and to Michael Pucylo, who provided legal advice on some of the more controversial matters in the story. Both individuals played a pivotal role in the revitalization of the EFCL and provided an important personal perspective of EFCL-related events.

My compliments to two writers: Vaughn Bowler and Michael Wanchuk. Their book, *Volunteers*, published in 1986, recounts the history of the EFCL and provides detailed coverage of each of the existing leagues. Their hard work and research materials were of great help. Above all, they provided me with the idea for this book, and the inspiration to complete it. I am also indebted to the many others along the way who continued to encourage me to write this book—community league and area council colleagues, friends, and my family. I am particularly indebted to my children, Kaitlyn and Mitchell, whose sense of youthful optimism, community-minded spirit, and volunteerism in our community have been a constant inspiration. The efforts of many such young folks on behalf of their community, and their focus on its welfare, is reassuring. It confirms that the essence of our humanity—to provide service so others will live better—will continue to light our way and lighten the load of the needy.

Finally yet importantly, I wish to thank University of Alberta Press, its director Linda Cameron and her staff for making the publication process smooth and enjoyable. The acquisitions editor, Michael Luski, patiently guided me through the publication process. Alan Brownoff was invaluable with picture selection, Denise Ahlefeldt with layout design, and Cathie Crooks with marketing. Jill Fallis merits my gratitude for her invaluable and extensive editing effort. Ken Tingley, a local historian who has published extensively, deserves my thanks for his guidance with the final editing of this manuscript. Allan Shute, who chronicled the history of the Riverdale area, also provided me with much appreciated guidance.

Mahatma Gandhi said, "Man becomes great exactly in the degree in which he works for the welfare of his fellow man." I hope that the following story inspires others to continue the decades-long network of community volunteers who have clearly demonstrated their greatness.

Introduction

*We live in a world in which we need to share
responsibility. It's easy to say "It's not my child,
not my community, not my world, not my problem."
Then there are those who see the need and respond.
I consider those people my heroes.*

— CHILDREN'S ENTERTAINER FRED ROGERS

As MINISTER OF COMMUNITY DEVELOPMENT with responsibility for volunteerism, it gives me great pleasure to provide this brief introduction to *Edmonton's Urban Villages: The Community League Movement*. Have you ever wondered why Edmonton is such a great city and how it became so? Well, this book will tell you about Edmonton's incredible legacy of volunteerism and the amazing role that our community leagues have played and continue to play in helping Edmonton succeed. It is very much about you and me and everyone who is, or ever was, an Edmontonian.

From the creation of our first community league in 1917 through to the 145 leagues that presently comprise the Edmonton Federation of Community Leagues (EFCL), it is clear that the community league movement dramatically influenced what, today, we know and love as our "City of Champions." Yet, inasmuch as it is the story of the EFCL, it is also an in depth look at Edmonton's history—its people, events, and activities that have shaped our very character as a community of many, beating as a heart of one. References to local, provincial, national, and international occurrences provide an insightful background and context within which our city has evolved, including our challenges and achievements.

Skillfully and flowingly written by respected author Dr. Ron Kuban, a most deserving recipient of the Queen's Golden Jubilee Medal for volunteerism, it depicts our city's growth from the days of early settlement through to a modern, diverse, and vibrant city which recently boasted the largest economic activity gains of any city in North America and a quality of life that has attracted international attention time and again. Along the way are many pleasant (and sometimes surprising) reminders of many of Edmonton's "firsts," all of which will amaze you and, I hope, reaffirm your commitment to this great city that so many of us proudly call home. Thank you to all the volunteers who were instrumental in the founding, development, and growth of the community league movement, and also to those who are currently engaged in continuing its legacy.

Now, I invite you to enjoy this literary and pictorial journey, revealing *Edmonton's Urban Villages*. I most certainly did!

GENE ZWOZDESKY, MINISTER (1994)
ALBERTA COMMUNITY DEVELOPMENT

EDMONTON'S GREATEST ASSET IS ITS PEOPLE. Their grassroots involvement, community focus, and voluntary spirit are well illustrated by Edmonton's community league movement.

The creation of the city's first community league, in 1917, heralded a movement that continues to grow strong. It has survived more than 87 years of change, and contributed extensively to all facets of life across our city, our region, and our province. The movement's accomplishments are a credit to thousands of city residents who volunteered their time, talent, and resources to ensure that their "community" becomes a great place to call home. As such, these volunteers, their community league, and the Edmonton Federation of Community Leagues (EFCL) have truly played a pivotal role in making Edmonton the great city that it is today—a "City of Champions."

The tradition continues, as every day at community events across the city Edmontonians continue to volunteer their valuable time and skills in support of community league programs. They are continuing a long and proud legacy of service.

On behalf of City Council and the citizens of Edmonton, I extend my sincere thanks to the volunteers who supported our city's community league movement. My thanks are also extended to Ron Kuban for having taken the initiative to record the history of our community league movement in *Edmonton's Urban Villages*.

STEPHEN MANDEL, MAYOR
CITY OF EDMONTON

THOSE WHO THINK HISTORY BOOKS tend to be nothing but a boring collection of names or dates should read this one. This book is fascinating from many perspectives. It talks about an organization—the Edmonton Federation of Community Leagues—which has a long history of loyally serving as a grassroots social movement. The storyline carries you from the laying of Edmonton's foundation, over one hundred years ago, through today and into the future. Along the way, it illustrates how the community league movement was instrumental in moulding the city of Edmonton into a vibrant and unique Canadian metropolis.

This story also illustrates that people, even in the role of volunteers, really do make a difference and along the way can shape the present and future. Repeatedly, one is awestruck by the "power of one," or the ability of one or a few individuals to enhance the welfare of so many. The amazing aspect is that this incredible movement continues to flourish after more than eighty-seven years of evolution, yet is still true to its founding principles.

On behalf of the Edmonton Federation of Community Leagues, I encourage you to read this fresh and flavourful story about the community league movement and the city that it helped to shape. This is an important addition to anyone's library, including mine.

SHANE BERGDAHL, PRESIDENT
EDMONTON FEDERATION OF COMMUNITY LEAGUES

Prologue

Growth is the only evidence of life.
— JOHN HENRY NEWMAN

DAY-TO-DAY OBLIGATIONS often focus our attention on the here and now, away from the far horizons of past and future. Yet amidst the hustle and bustle of life we must take the time to pause and celebrate the past, frame the future, or do both. The centenary of the City of Edmonton in 2004 and of the Province of Alberta in 2005 are perfect opportunities to rejoice the incredible achievements of countless oft-unsung heroes. These are the volunteers who over almost nine decades established and maintained the community league or neighbourhood structure that enhances the quality of life for Edmonton's residents. These heroes provided Edmonton with a unique lasting legacy that is described in this book.

In this regard, the book you are about to read is unique. It tells the history of a city through the achievements of its ordinary citizens. Each chapter begins with a broad chronicle of an era in the growth of the city of Edmonton and focuses on the events that unfolded at the municipal and (occasionally) at the provincial level. This provides context for the more detailed narrative in the rest of the chapter, about Edmonton's community leagues and the unique social movement that transformed the city. The city and the movement influenced each other and over time became intertwined, almost interdependent, especially in times of great communal need.

Edmonton confronted and overcame its share of challenges. Natural disasters such as floods, storms, landslides, and a tornado as well as explosions, major fires, dangerous goods spills, the threat of rebellion (Louis Riel), wars, political strife, financial hardships, business failures, and a variety of other calamities tested the community and its various organizations. Yet Edmonton grew from a tiny settlement to become a prominent trading fort, a town, a city, and a provincial capital for Alberta. In the end, the people of Edmonton passed the test of time with flying colours.

Edmonton's civic leaders, who in the early decades were predominantly the giants of local industry or commerce, often receive credit for the city's numerous achievements. In time, the ranks of these civic leaders also included those who held public office and more recently those who excelled in the arts or in sports. These individuals had a vision, a sense of a grand purpose, the will to act, the force of leadership, and the stamina to bring their dream to fruition. They brought to bear the force of their religious, cultural, or political beliefs and left an indelible imprint on the city, the province, and Canada. Their accomplishments became history, and their names now adorn many of Edmonton's streets, bridges, buildings, trophies, and the Hall of Fame at city hall.

In this respect, Edmonton is much like many places in the world. Unlike most other settlements, however, Edmonton had an advantage: it was built as a collection of "urban villages," each with its own solidly entrenched community spirit. As such, it grew and matured one neighbourhood at a time through a grassroots movement with distinct building blocks—community leagues.

The concept for Edmonton's community league movement came from Rochester, New York: it was a replica of the City Club. Such clubs, first formed in the early 1900s, provided a counterbalance to the pervasive power of aggressive municipal politicians or developers and allowed private citizens more say in their local governance. In time, the original concept evolved to a more politically focused and socialistic form. For Edmonton, however, the movement became a unique approach to citizen participation in community affairs. Unlike the City Club movement, Edmonton's community leagues stood the test of time.

From their inception, these leagues augmented the abilities and capacity of civic leaders. The leagues mobilized and maintained a substantial group of community-minded volunteers who helped monitor, shape, promote, and maintain a steady improvement in the local quality of life. For more than

Donald Ross coal mine, 1890.
City of Edmonton Archives EA 10-1180.

federal government to settle the recently surveyed lands. According to the Dominion Lands Act of 1872, settlers could claim up to 65 hectares (160 acres, or a quarter section) of land, for ten dollars and a commitment to live on and work the land for three years. In 1882, when the Dominion Land Survey reached the Fort Edmonton area, the process of land claims became easier, with restrictions on claim-jumping and the provision of a legal structure. Settlers were further enticed to the area by the westward push of the railway.

The Canadian Pacific Railway, or CPR, was continuing its cross-Canada expansion. Edmonton residents expected that by 1875 the railway would make its way first through Fort Edmonton and then the Yellowhead Pass on its way to the Pacific Ocean. A few years later, in 1881 when it reached Winnipeg, the railway brought a flood of new settlers who generated an economic boom. Though Fort Edmonton residents watched and waited in great anticipation, crushing disappointment followed. The CPR announced its decision to route the railway line along the southern Prairie region. Disappointment grew when in 1883 the rail line reached Fort Edmonton's southern rival: Fort Calgary. The arrival of the railway placed Fort Calgary as the new heart of the western Prairies,

First train to arrive in south Edmonton, November 25, 1891.
City of Edmonton Archives EA 10-2760.

isolated Fort Edmonton, and resulted in the disappearance of many small settlements between the two forts. Nevertheless, Fort Edmonton had a calling that
sustained it despite its isolation: it served as the gateway to the north.

The arrival in 1874 of the North West Mounted Police, the forerunner of
today's Royal Canadian Mounted Police (RCMP), helped re-establish law and
order, which was previously a concern. Before the arrival of the Mounted Police,
representatives of the Hudson's Bay Company served to maintain law and order.
Their ability to perform this role suffered during the lawlessness that the
whiskey trade generated in its wake, especially during its heyday from 1869 to
1874. Not surprisingly, the establishment of law and order (under federal jurisdiction) led to the development of the community and its physical and
communal infrastructures. During the 1870s and 1880s, the pattern of life for
the inhabitants of the small fort started to become more structured and organized. Within a short period, the residents achieved many key milestones and
constructed vital structures. These included:

- the introduction of steamboats, in 1875, to provide river service along the North Saskatchewan River between Winnipeg and Fort Edmonton
- the arrival, in 1879, of the Dominion telegraph line to the south bank of the river (with Alex Taylor as its first operator)
- the first official post office at the fort, in 1878, with Richard Hardisty as its first postmaster
- Alberta's first newspaper, the *Bulletin*, established in 1880 by Frank Oliver and Alex Taylor
- the first cable ferry across the North Saskatchewan River, in 1881, by John Walter
- the establishment by Matthew McCauley in 1881 of the first public school in Alberta (which until 1884 was funded by private subscriptions)
- the introduction by Alex Taylor in 1886 of the telephone to area residents (Nearly twenty years later, Taylor sold his telephone business to the City of Edmonton, which operated the phone company [Edmonton Telephone Corporation, later Ed Tel] until its sale in the 1990s to Alberta Government Telephones [AGT])

In 1891, Alex Taylor provided the growing community with electricity generated through his coal-burning boiler. During that year, the Calgary & Edmonton (C&E) Railway finally reached Edmonton. Well, not quite. Its northern terminal was on the south bank of the river, in South Edmonton, and that became a sore point for the booming settlement of Fort Edmonton. Nevertheless, the arrival of the railway to the gates of Fort Edmonton heralded a new boom and a new wave of settlers.

By then, there were many great leaders, the movers and shakers of the community, who achieved many feats. They included Malcolm Alexander Groat, who arrived in Fort Edmonton in 1861 from Fort Garry, Manitoba. He served as the second-in-command for HBC chief factor William J. Christie, and he eventually settled the lands that are currently bounded by 121st Street, the river, 149th Street, and 111th Avenue. He donated some of his land to the Catholic and Anglican churches, which were the first to exist outside the fort. He also donated his time and effort by founding the Northern Alberta Pioneers and Old Timers Association.

John A. McDougall was another community-minded pioneer. He arrived in Fort Edmonton in 1877 and began to trade in furs and supplies, making a number of trips between the fort and Winnipeg. Two years later, he settled in Fort Edmonton and opened a trading store. Later, in partnership with another community-minded entrepreneur, Richard Secord, he successfully built a number of businesses, including a department store and a real estate business. His public service includes serving as chair of the public school board, alderman, president of the Board of Trade, mayor (twice), Liberal MLA, and member of the University of Alberta Senate. (Both McDougall and Secord have descendants in modern Edmonton. John McDougall is head of the Alberta Research Council, and Richard Secord is a distinguished lawyer specializing in aboriginal and environmental matters.)

Alex Taylor's entrepreneurial successes left a significant impact on the community. The prosperous businessperson also served as the Dominion weatherman, postmaster, clerk of the court, and the chairman of the school board. Yet he also found time to serve his community and became a significant role model for dignity and courage (having lost in later years the use of both arms).

Matthew McCauley, another example of a great entrepreneur who distinguished himself in business and public life, came to Fort Edmonton in 1881 from a farm in Fort Saskatchewan to operate the first livery stable in Edmonton, a stagecoach and mail service. He also organized the fort's first school and became the chairman of the school board and a trustee. In 1892, he became the first mayor of the newly incorporated town of Edmonton and served three terms in that capacity, later assuming the role of delegate to the Northwest Territories Assembly in Regina, MLA in Alberta's first assembly, and eventually warden of the newly established federal penitentiary in Edmonton.

Indeed, during the 1870s and 1880s, the community at and around Fort Edmonton was growing steadily and life was becoming more and more structured. Yet one major achievement eluded it and appeared to threaten its continued success. A major problem for the fort was its location on the north side of the river, the higher of the two banks. This fact of geography prevented it from direct connection to the main lifeline of the time: the railway.

When the CPR, which had made great strides in its westward expansion, reached Fort Calgary in 1883, this shifted the balance of commerce from Fort Edmonton to its rival in the south and raised demands to link the two by rail.

2

The Community Gives a Voice

1915–1929

If I am not for myself, who will?
If I am only for myself, what am I?
If not now, when?

— THE TALMUD

EDMONTON AT THE TURN OF THE TWENTIETH CENTURY was prosperous and its population optimistic about its future.[1] No one expected the hardships that would befall it over subsequent decades. Yet the city managed to survive these hardships and to create a unique social organization that helped shape its future in unimaginable ways. This organization, transplanted from the eastern United States and transformed into a made-in-Edmonton institute, became a profound social movement. The story begins with social conditions in the city and the state of its development.

Despite its relative isolation, or perhaps because of its existence as the gateway to the North, Edmonton remained attractive to waves of immigrants who flocked in, primarily via the railway, to swell the city's population by 30 percent in 1907 and again in 1908, so that at the start of 1909 Edmonton's population had reached nearly 15,000. However, while prosperity grew, these hardy and still few-in-number folk were responsible for a heavy financial burden. They financed the burgeoning local infrastructure—streets, sidewalks, sewer system, telephone, and many other services—for their city's current population as well as the thousands expected to flock to it in the upcoming years. Financial difficulties on the other side of the continent made this responsibility, demanding enough by itself, significantly more onerous. In April 1907, fuelled by a wave of panic, the New York Stock Exchange tumbled. This situation rippled through other stock markets and led to a continent-wide recession.

The task of managing Edmonton's growth amid these financial woes was in the hands of W. A. Griesbach. Nicknamed the "Boy Mayor" for his age of twenty-seven, Griesbach had his hands full. The city's infrastructure was still in its infancy, with little to support the rapid growth and the demands of the growing populace. For example, the task of sweeping and tidying the town hall fell to the police department, and the plumbing department had the responsibility for a baby whose mother was dying and whose father was dead due to typhoid—no other agency was available for the task. And so it went, with different civic agencies covering off roles that would usually be addressed by more specialized organizations. Church groups were available to assist, but the limited presence of community-based voluntary or not-for-profit organizations only made the situation more difficult.

Establishing a workable public transit system continued to be a major objective, with Griesbach trying to raise the necessary funds through debentures or bonds. Because these were not readily available at the New York money markets, the city secured its funding through the London markets, at a heavy cost.

Another long-standing issue for the city was the transition from coal to gas as a source of heating.[2] This, too, was on the agenda of Griesbach and his council. They reviewed a number of options and presentations by large companies, but eventually refused them all. The big corporations of the time had earned the reputation of being high-handed and dishonest in their business affairs. The practice of unbridled competition, lack of regulations, squandering of limited resources due to duplication of facilities, and unethical behaviour, especially where bribes were the norm in business practices, further added to the public mistrust.

Edmonton and Strathcona were primarily business communities that catered to the needs of pioneers. Development and real estate were hot items during this period, with nearly half of the almost 200 local businesses in Edmonton being real estate agents. Many others without formal registration as agents dabbled in the purchase and sale of real estate in hopes of making a quick profit.

The year 1907 saw much real estate activity in both Edmonton and Strathcona. The former established new subdivisions including Belvedere, Cromdale, Dwyer, Earnscliff, Ellerman, Lynwood, North Jasper Place, Richmond, and Santa Rosa. When Strathcona was incorporated as a city on March 15, 1907, its boundaries were enlarged by nearly 16 square kilometres (6 square miles). Although much of this land was either undeveloped or farmed, it nevertheless allowed room for expansion. A month later, on April 6, when Premier A. C. Rutherford announced the establishment of the University of Alberta within Strathcona, developers rushed to secure and develop the land around it. A new subdivision, University Park, quickly arose within Strathcona. Another development, Grandview Heights, formed outside that city's boundary.

Easier times seemed to have arrived in 1907 Edmonton, reflected by the opening of two more theatres and the presence of an increasing number of cars along the city's few paved roads. Edmonton's residents, determined to spend their tax money in various business enterprises, convinced city council to start the first municipal golf course in Canada, which became the Victoria Municipal course. Another enterprise, the Diamond Park stadium became the centre for Edmonton sporting activities such as baseball and soccer.

However, by July of that year, financial hardships began to threaten the city's ability to deliver its few services or establish new ones. The city treasurer announced that Edmonton had spent all its money and could not raise more from the local banks. Taxpayers, pleased with earlier increases in the value of their property, were nevertheless unhappy with the subsequent increase in their tax mill rate from 10.5 to 13.5. Another part of Edmonton's solution to its financial woes was to sell $679,000 worth of debentures. This strategy alleviated some of its immediate financial difficulties, but created an extra cost because the debentures brought only ninety-three cents on the dollar.

The year 1907 was supposed to be prosperous, and expectations were that Edmonton would at last have a new telephone system and a street railway as its public transportation system. The failure of the city to achieve these two expected goals resulted in the defeat of Mayor Griesbach and his council, and John A. McDougall became the new mayor. A capable business person in his own right, McDougall set out to tackle the city's financial and social problems systematically. Times were tough in the winter of 1907–08, and many families took shelter in hundreds of tents that lined the river flats and the city's boundaries. Most relied on their own resources for support but at least eighteen families depended on public relief.

A year earlier, a new player had entered public life—the University of Alberta. Soon thereafter Premier Rutherford, a McGill University graduate, secured Dr. Henry Marshall Tory, also a McGill alumnus, as the university's first president. The university's first year involved forty-five students and four professors. Aside from education, the university soon became the centre for diverse activities involving adult education, the arts, and the community at large.

In the meanwhile, Edmonton was growing. By 1908, there were fire, police, and waterworks departments, seven public schools, one separate school, two colleges, and five hospitals. Edmonton's population, totalling 18,500 at year-end, enjoyed expanded civic utilities and services—many of which materialized thanks to the energetic effort of the business-oriented mayor and council. However, this growth continued to increase the cost (and value) of real estate so that, by 1909, properties along Jasper Avenue and 101st Street were selling at $10,000 per foot (30 cm) of frontage.

In 1910, Edmonton's mill rate rose to 17 and its assessment total climbed by $5 million from the previous year's total of $20 million. Due to its expanding population, the city annexed approximately 1,940 hectares (4,800 acres), almost doubling its size. Among its new subdivisions were Calder, Eastwood, Fairview, Groat Estate, Hempriggs, Inglewood, Kensington, Lauderdale, Northcote, Norwood, Parkdale, Rosslyn, Sherbrooke, Wellington, Westwood, Woodcroft, and Woodland.[3]

Seven out of ten city residents had been born in Canada, the United States, or the British Isles. But the population was evolving, gradually showing greater and greater diversity: French-speaking (3%), German and Scandinavian (8%), and Slavic (15%), with the remainder Belgian, Dutch, Hungarian, Greek, Italian, Chinese, and African-American.

Nineteen-twelve was Edmonton's all-time boom year. By year's end, the population had grown from 31,000 to 50,000, spurring a previously unparalleled publicly funded development in roads, buildings, and public structures. However, once again this growth came at an incredible cost—a debt load that took the next thirty-five years to repay.

Private-based development was not far behind, and real estate agents were having a heyday. A notable case is the 59-hectare (145-acre) Hagmann estate, of the future that was slow to materialize. Though the post-war years heralded many changes including women's emancipation, the abolition of prohibition, and many technological advances, Edmonton's infrastructure hardly changed. The city's population in 1926 was almost 7,000 people fewer than its 1914 record-high number. Growth was mostly in the service sector, with no new major industry added to the city's roster. Few buildings were constructed, and the city streets remained essentially as they were at the start of the war. It was a time of great need, increasing public expectation, and the growth of diverse social organizations and movements. One such movement was the City Club.

かつ かつ

Originated in the late 1800s, the City Club movement and its Social Center program took form in the eastern United States. By 1909, Rochester, N.Y., had an established club. From there, the club began spreading in the early 1910s across the eastern United States to cities like Boston, Chicago, Cleveland, Milwaukee, New York, and Philadelphia, among others. Established as a club for men who wanted to meet regularly and discuss local issues, meetings occurred over lunch and became a forum for individuals to explore a variety of topics. Membership was set at one dollar, but many clubs decided to waive that fee, directing instead that every man who attended and paid for his lunch automatically became a member. A few decades later, women also joined the club and eventually became active in the City Club structure.

The City Clubs were a forum for public education and community-focused dialogue. Invited speakers made presentations on key topics of interest and were available to answer questions from those attending. In time the discussion of local issues evolved to include issues of more national and international flavour. Although some of the clubs operated as a social club, many also operated as watchdogs over their community activities or as clearinghouses for discussion on local issues. Common philosophical tenets, such as more inclusive use of public school facilities by community organizations, guided the clubs. (This became a major issue for Edmonton community leagues.)

The City Club concept and especially its Social Center movement were still in their infancy in the United States when George M. Hall, the city's industrial commissioner, transplanted the concept to Edmonton. Hall, who had

George M. Hall was born in Providence, Rhode Island, where he first became involved in education and politics. He apprenticed as a correspondent for the *Providence Journal* and the *Tribune*, and served four years as superintendent of schools. In 1906, he moved to Winnipeg, where he worked for two Winnipeg newspapers and for five years served with the Winnipeg Industrial Bureau. He also studied industrial development and publicity under the mentorship of Charles Roland, Winnipeg's industrial commissioner. In August 1912, Hall moved to Edmonton to become its industrial commissioner. During his first year there, he helped prepare the Morell and Nicols report on the city's planning. The report's most lasting recommendation was the grouping and relocation of large industrial development to areas outside the city. These recommendations were intended to eliminate heavy smoke and preserve the river valley's beautiful appearance.

In 1913, Hall's position title changed to industrial and publicity commissioner. During that year, he published *The Edmonton Way: Public Parks System of Edmonton*. A year later, city council restructured its administration and abolished Hall's position. By 1915, he was running the Edmonton Industrial and Development Bureau with Leslie A. Smart.

Hall and his family moved into the area known as Jasper Place. This was a neighbourhood with virtually no infrastructure and isolated from the core of the city. It had a two-room schoolhouse on a questionable foundation, no electricity or sewerage, and only limited streetcar access. In 1916, in response to these conditions, the neighbourhood formed the Jasper Place Rate Payers (JPRP) Association. In May 1917, Hall travelled to the United States to research the Social Center movement and its City Clubs. On his return, he integrated the JPRP Association with the horticultural society to form Edmonton's first community league, now known as the Crestwood Community League. Hall served as the league's president for its first three years.

funding secured from both the city and the school boards, the EFCL improved and maintained ice rinks within the various communities in exchange for providing free-of-charge skating to school-aged children. It also ensured that the city provided a block of land to each of the leagues, to be used for recreational purposes. This was an extension of the precedent set by the 142nd Street District League.

Much of the EFCL's work in its early years was achieved through three standing committees: educational, civic, and recreation. The educational committee arranged for speakers as requested by the leagues. It also coordinated the lending of the EFCL movie projector to any league that required it. The civic committee made presentations to council and city agencies on behalf of the federation or its member leagues, as requested by these leagues. The recreation committee organized and conducted inter-league sports activities or events. For example, the recreation committee helped organize speed skating, baseball, tennis, bowling, hockey, basketball, football, track and field, and physical drills. From their inception these committees provided the EFCL and its leagues with an informal yet loud voice on civic development issues.

The leagues did not always choose to take action through the federation; occasionally they acted unilaterally to secure their own position or meet a unique need. However, when coordinated action was required between the leagues, it was achieved through the EFCL, which in reality was "owned" by its member leagues. Each of them sent a representative to the EFCL meetings. Quorum was established by the presence of a representative from the majority of the leagues. By far, the EFCL's greatest influence was through its establishment of broad guidelines regarding policies or activities.

Meeting by meeting, issue by issue, the leagues and their federation began to establish their presence as a voice of the people on civic and recreational matters. Their voice was heard, time and again, on issues such as taxes, roads, mail service, recreation, slot machines, community clean-up, education, policing, and even the city zoo.

The leagues' relationship with local schools started early in their existence, and access to school facilities and rink funding quickly became key points of contention. The leagues needed a place for their meetings and programs, and they sought the after-hours use of the local school facilities. It was provided grudgingly and not without conflict. For example, on January 16, 1925, the *Edmonton Bulletin* reported on a meeting of the public school board held the night

Children on a slide, circa 1913.
City of Edmonton Archives EA 509-10.

before to discuss the holding of community league dances on Saturday nights at the schools. Apparently, after much debate and a closely split vote, a motion to allow dances was defeated, thanks to Dr. T. J. Johnson, a school trustee, who complained strenuously about "dancing and card playing." He did not support the argument that these events generated revenues toward community activities such as building ice rinks and conducting recreational programs for children.

By the late 1920s, rental fees were established and set at one dollar for school rooms and three dollars for assembly halls (or gymnasiums). But, by January 1929, these fees were on the rise. The superintendent of schools, G. A. McKee, was invited to a meeting of the EFCL to talk about educational problems in Edmonton. (Two months earlier, the EFCL was reported in the *Bulletin* as expressing concern about teachers being overworked and about low student marks, which averaged 33 percent). The agenda also included the school budget for the year and the proposed increases to the rental fee paid by the leagues. In time, these increases proved prohibitive for community league programs and generated the push toward the establishment of community halls.

Ice rinks, in great demand, were also a great challenge for the leagues that used volunteers and fund-drives to establish and maintain them. The leagues were already becoming increasingly involved in local sport programs. By the late 1920s, more than 4,000 boys were being trained in hockey, with many trophies being donated to boys' and men's hockey, girls' and men's basketball, men's football, and speed skating. But funding for these rinks was an issue.

Nearly four years earlier, at a meeting involving G. F. McNally, supervisor of public schools for the province, the EFCL had addressed the matter of school curriculum and funding for the use of league-built ice rinks by schoolchildren. The EFCL objected to the school board funding (in amounts ranging from $135 to $250) of commercial enterprises, especially when these were located in districts where leagues had developed their own rinks. By the end of 1925, the school board had agreed to pay the leagues a lesser lump-sum amount than the commercial properties for the cost-free use of league rinks by schoolchildren. In November 1925, the city began to provide annual grants of $125 in cash and free utilities to the league-operated rinks.

Rink maintenance and its cost were also concerns. In January 1926, based on the recommendations of city engineer A. W. Haddow, a graduated annual grant system for community rink maintenance was established, based on the size of the ice surface, presence of lighting and dressing room(s), the height of the fence around the rink, and other factors. The grant helped the leagues to upgrade their rinks.

A number of other issues occupied the leagues during the second half of the 1920s. They pushed for local improvements such as roads and sidewalks, they opposed tax increases, and they asked for the abolition and removal of the 225 slot machines that existed in Edmonton during 1924. (A similar campaign was waged in the late 1990s.) A year later, the leagues were involved in a tree-planting campaign, and in late 1926 the EFCL "registered an energetic protest at the proposal of the city to levy an annual license fee of $15 on all skating rinks in the city" (reported in the *Edmonton Bulletin* November 13, 1926). Better mail service became an issue at the request of the Highland Community League, as did funding for the creation of the zoo at Borden Park.

During April and May 1926, the *Edmonton Bulletin* (and later the *Edmonton Journal*) sponsored a citywide "Clean-up, Plant-up, Paint-up" campaign, supported by fourteen of the existing community leagues. The *Bulletin* offered

$175 in cash prizes to the top three leagues with the best relative improvement. The city supplied the leagues with native trees, free of charge. The campaign lasted a number of weeks and received a great deal of coverage in the *Bulletin*, which raved about the success of the campaign and the leagues' effort within it.

Policing was also an issue for the leagues. The January 24, 1924, issue of the *Bulletin* noted that Edmonton police had responded to vandalism complaints at several community league rinks. The police representatives reportedly caught the culprits, whose parents "made good the damage."

Amid these issues, the EFCL became more and more politically active. On December 29, 1925, the *Bulletin* reported that the EFCL was seeking representation on a variety of municipal boards including the hospital, welfare, library, and the exhibition grounds. In early 1926, the EFCL began assessing the possibility of its entry into civic politics through the selection or endorsement of its own candidates for city council or school board. After much debate, the federation deferred the matter to its twenty-four individual community leagues. On November 13, 1926, the *Bulletin* reported that a large majority of these leagues had turned down the proposal to enter civic politics due to the perceived limitation imposed by the EFCL mandate. A month later, during an election campaign, the leagues organized an all-candidates' forum at the Rose Theatre and grilled candidates on their stance regarding a number of issues. The consensus was in favour of including EFCL representatives on the various civic boards.

The involvement of the EFCL in civic politics arose again at the federation's January 17, 1929, meeting, which ironically occurred in council chambers. Lengthy discussion of the topic concluded in a decision by a two-thirds majority against entering civic politics. (This topic arose repeatedly during the life of the EFCL, often with the same results.) Nevertheless, many leagues held meetings at election time to which all candidates were invited. These were of value for the community residents as well as the candidates, as illustrated by the following story by H. P. Brown as reported in the *Bulletin*:

In one election, a candidate decided to call his own meeting, which proved unwise as he subsequently informed a community league audience: "Only two people came, a woman and myself; it was a large and enthusiastic meeting—she was large and I was enthusiastic."

The future of the leagues in the 1920s was indeed fraught with challenges. Yet both they and their federation held as they grew in number, activity, and recognition. But a greater challenge—the Great Depression—was just around the corner, and it was to test the community league movement and its volunteers, and their capacity to serve area residents and their city.

No act of kindness, however small, is ever wasted.

— AESOP

wheat, resulting from tariffs imposed on wheat by the U.S. government in protection of its own producers.

That year, the price of various grains fell significantly.[2] No. 1 Northern Wheat declined from $1.11 to $0.34 per bushel; oats and barley fell similarly to 11 and 13 cents. In 1931, prices again declined to 23.5 cents a bushel for No. 1 Northern Wheat, 10 cents for oats, and 12.5 cents for barley. The drop in prices impacted all aspects of life in the Edmonton area. Local farmers reduced grain growing areas and diversified into mixed farming. Many began to reduce or eliminate expenses, including farm machinery, stock, and the seasonal farm workers upon whom they typically relied for help. The reduction in consumption of goods and services rippled across Canada and resulted in factory closures, restricted lending by banks, countless layoffs, and the reduction of capital projects.

Construction in Edmonton and area followed the declining grain prices. The few major construction projects during 1930 to 1936 included the Birks Building and the Natural Resources Building (both completed in 1930), the Masonic Hall (1931), and Canada Packers (1936). Residential construction fared no better. Building permits, in 1929 valued at a record $5.67 million, dropped to $4.3 million in 1930 and further down to $428,000 in 1933. In 1938, building permits totalled $2.8 million—half the 1929 value.

The financial woes compounded when another catastrophe—drought—spread across the prairies. The Great Dry soon turned the prairies into a dust bowl, and vast stretches of farmland became covered by desert-like sand. For a while, farmers optimistically continued to till their land, which made matters worse. Then, in droves, they left the land, abandoning farmsteads, farm implements, and their lifestyle.

The rapidly declining state of the economy created vast numbers of unemployed, who roamed across Canada in the hope of finding work that would sustain them and their family.[3] Times were tough and opportunities few. The private sector could not sustain employment, and the task fell on the shoulders of the various orders of government, which lacked the necessary capital and organizational infrastructure to support those who were unemployed. Hastily established make-work projects cropped up everywhere, but did not meet the rapidly growing ranks of those looking for work. This bred resentment, tension, and anger.

Depression era huts on the grounds below the Macdonald Hotel. City of Edmonton Archives EA 160-325.

The first public demonstration against the deteriorating conditions occurred on December 31, 1929, when about 100 men marched on city hall to demand work. Two days later, 750 of them registered at a newly created office of the provincial government and began clearing brush in the local area. A year later, the ranks of the unemployed in Edmonton had swelled to include 5,171 men who were registered with the city relief officer. This placed tremendous financial pressure on the city's coffers, yet the commitment to continue the support for those in need held. Mayor J. M. Douglas declared: "We are endeavouring to prevent starvation and privation. We must continue to give relief and we must afford it. We cannot allow our people to starve, even if it means an increase in the tax rate."[4]

As time advanced, the ranks of the unemployed and their plight continued to increase substantially, in Edmonton and elsewhere across Canada. Public gatherings and marches highlighted the need for relief. Initially, these events were peaceful, but as the need and demand for assistance grew far beyond the capacity of government, tension mounted and hostility flared. By May 1931, city hall required close protection during council meetings.

In May, the city began to provide meals of porridge to unemployed single men. The city's kitchen served an average of 2,500 bowls of porridge and remained open until 1938! Yet this served only as a stopgap measure and did not meet the growing demand for relief. On June 10, 1931, a large contingent of the unemployed stormed city hall, demanding immediate assistance. This event, and the flood of unemployed who came to Edmonton to seek relief, generated much concern for Mayor Douglas, city council, and Premier J. E. Brownlee. The premier, fearing the increasing influence of the Communist Party on the unemployed, requested assistance from the military. A contingent of sixty-plus mounted troops arrived from Calgary's Lord Strathcona Horse and took position at the Prince of Wales armouries.

While the federal, provincial, and municipal governments scrambled to maintain order, a coalition of community groups began to organize their own relief effort. This coalition, organized by the Edmonton Trades and Labour Council, included representatives from the local Alberta Federation of Labour, the Canadian Legion, the Chamber of Commerce, Civil Servants Association, Council of Women, the Edmonton diocese of the Roman Catholic Church, the Hope Mission, Ministerial Association, Edmonton Public School Board, the Red Cross, the Women's Labour Council, and the Edmonton Federation of Community Leagues (EFCL). An executive committee for this coalition, elected on June 26, 1931, had the mandate to facilitate better cooperation between the city's relief effort and that of the private agencies.

The start of World War II, in September 1939, was almost surreal for those in Edmonton who were still recovering from the Depression.[5] Many people had suffered tremendous hardship, deprivation, or sorrow during those rough years of drought, unemployment, and financial limitation. Yet Edmonton and northern Alberta had fared relatively better than southern Alberta and much better than the farmers and residents of Saskatchewan. Moreover, not everyone experienced the Depression in the same manner and with the same results. In his book, Edmonton: A History, James MacGregor observed:

> Thinking back to the depression, we are apt to remember only the dramatic, the hunger, the bread lines and the Bennett Buggies, and we are apt to paint an excessively black picture. What we are apt to forget is how the grim conditions welded everyone, whether employed or

unemployed, into a new camaraderie. Traits of kindliness, helpfulness and neighbourliness, sometimes dulled during prosperous times, shone forth anew during the depression. What we might forget too is that many thousands of people, who were lucky enough or good enough to keep their jobs, hardly felt its sting. (p. 248)

The Depression also saw changes to the social infrastructure of society. Like many other Canadian communities, Edmonton gained through the creation or enhancement of many socially focused organizations, including the EFCL. Those who lived at that time across the Prairies demonstrated a spirit of volunteerism that is readily visible today and that still sets them apart from other Canadians.

In its own way, the Depression also served as a cultural melting pot that brought together many cultures, ideologies, and lifestyles into the large communities like Edmonton. Migration to urban centres, the search for employment, growing communication networks, and travel, as well as the need for mutual support from diverse groups of people, facilitated this process. One of the signs of the time and immigration was the construction in 1938 of the Al Raschid mosque, established on 108th Avenue to become the first mosque in Canada.

When Ottawa placed the Edmonton Regiment (renamed the Loyal Edmonton Regiment after the Battle of Ortona, in 1943, and nicknamed the "Loyal Eddies") on alert, on September 1, 1939, the Depression was showing signs of ending. So was the drought condition that had complicated the economic woes across the Prairies. Things were starting to return to normal. By 1938, the value of building permits in Edmonton had risen to $2,806,000 from the 1933 low of $428,000. Then the war came and left its own mark on life.

On September 3, 1939, following Germany's invasion of Poland, England declared war on Germany. A week later, Canada too declared war and began the massive effort of recruitment and war production, catapulting Canada's economy from the remnants of the Depression. Eager recruits lined Jasper Avenue and flocked to army headquarters at the Prince of Wales Armouries. Not until the invasion of Belgium and Holland on May 10, 1940, and the fall of Paris on June 14, however, did the war finally take on a more real, demanding, and worrisome shape. The likely invasion of England was a great concern for Canada.

In the period between the two world wars, the capacity of the Canadian army continued to deteriorate despite warnings from key people, including Edmonton's former "Boy Mayor," Major General W. A. Griesbach. Following the declaration of war, Canada began a rapid program of rearmament, recruitment, and training. To that end, Edmonton made a valuable contribution.

Recruitment was relatively easy, given years of Depression-based unemployment and the emotional rush to join the war for "King and country." Edmonton's per capita enlistment proved to be among the highest in Canada, sending recruits to all three services—army, navy, and air force. The Loyal Edmonton Regiment—the successor to the Edmonton-based Forty-Ninth Battalion—was rapidly filling its ranks through recruitment drives across Edmonton, which netted 450 of its original strength of 800. The rest came from Peace River, Red Deer, Vegreville, and Wetaskiwin. In time, the regiment proved itself in many battlefields across Europe and did Edmonton proud. (During the force reduction that occurred after the war, the regiment became the Fourth Battalion of the Princess Patricia's Canadian Light Infantry.)

Edmonton's contribution also extended to the navy and air force. HMCS Nonsuch was established in 1923 in an abandoned Hudson's Bay Company stable in Rossdale (at 102nd Street and 97th Avenue), and it became a focal point for Edmonton's residents who wanted to serve in the Canadian Navy. Many others, frustrated by Canada's initial shortage of naval vessels, rushed to England's aid by joining the Royal Navy.

One of Edmonton's most significant contributions to the war effort centred on Blatchford Field, the airport named after Kenny Blatchford, who served as Edmonton's mayor and the federal member for East Edmonton. The air terminal and hangars had become legendary during earlier decades because of numerous pilots such as "Wop" May, Punch Dickins, Matt Berry, Leigh Brintnell, Grant McConachie, George Gorman, Roy Brown, Keith Tailyour, and Jimmy Bell. Some made their name as bush pilots opening routes to the North, while others distinguished themselves during World War I. Regardless, these aviators served to promote flying, and they established Edmonton as a major hub for air services.

Upon the start of the war, the Edmonton Exhibition ground was once again conscripted for the war effort.[6] During World War I, the army used it,

An aerial view of Blatchford Field, 1936.
City of Edmonton Archives EA 10-3181-57-1.

but during World War II, the facilities were at the disposal of the air force. No. 2 Manning Depot became the primary centre for aviators, who arrived from all corners of the British Commonwealth for air training. To meet the sudden and extensive demand for training space and accommodations, the Royal Canadian Air Force also took control of the University of Alberta residences and conducted some training in its facilities.

After the Japanese attack on Pearl Harbor on December 7, 1941, the American presence in Edmonton grew to monumental proportions, starting with the decision on February 14, 1942, to build the Alaska Highway. It took nine months to complete the 2,450-kilometre (1,523-mile) highway with the help of 17,000 civilians, more than 10,000 U.S. troops, 7,000 pieces of rolling equipment, 54 Canadian and American contractors, $139 million, and unquestionable determination. The American troops established their headquarters in the area around 127th Street and 114th Avenue, where they built a hospital, residences, offices, and more. (After the war, the area's community leagues used some of these facilities.)

The presence of U.S. troops in Edmonton placed a great strain on the local housing market as well as other services. On the other hand, their presence

An incident during November 1942 serves as an example of the many benefits American troops provided to Edmonton residents. On Sunday, November 15, Edmonton and area received a record snowfall of 50 centimetres (19 1/2 inches). Drifts, waist-deep in the city, were nearly 4.5 metres (15 feet) high in surrounding areas. To make matters worse, the city had no snow removal equipment, and traffic ground to a halt. To the delight of the city's residents, United States Air Force troops and Alaska Highway crews who were in the city pitched in to clear the snow. Within two days the roads were again passable.

contributed greatly to the local economy through employment and the construction of numerous structures.

The project and Edmonton received a tremendous boost of resources following the Japanese attack on Dutch Harbor, Alaska, on June 3, 1942. That attack, following closely on the experience of Pearl Harbor, accelerated the United States's determination to protect Alaska. Two days after the Dutch Harbour attack, the Americans began a massive airlift of men and material to Alaska, and Edmonton's Blatchford Field became a stopover destination for refuelling and maintenance. By then, Edmonton was already becoming a hub for aircraft maintenance and repair, including many aircraft damaged during the Battle of Britain and the war over Europe.

This growth in air activity mirrored the growing demand for farm products, which helped to rejuvenate the farming sector so devastated by the Depression and triggered the development of Edmonton's business sector. Despite the recruitment of men and women for the war effort in other locations, Edmonton's population grew, from around 90,000 in 1939 to more than 93,800 in 1941 and over 113,100 in 1946.

Year by year, Edmonton's and Alberta's economy grew stronger.[7] The economy also benefited from the growth of coal mining in western Alberta and metal mining (mostly gold) that came through Edmonton from the North. Prosperity was starting to return, and with it came hope for the future. On May 8, 1945, Edmonton's residents celebrated Victory in Europe (VE) Day. It was a

The Queen Elizabeth Pool, Edmonton's first, circa 1930.
City of Edmonton Archives EA 10-1152.

subdued celebration in comparison to Victory in Japan (VJ) Day, which occurred nearly three months later on August 15. Finally, on October 6, 1945, the troops of the Loyal Edmonton Regiment returned home by train. A new chapter was about to start for them and their fellow Edmonton residents.

Returning veterans found their city and their society profoundly changed. Enhanced earning power for men and women had increased confidence and created opportunities for recreation and entertainment. The thousands of women who stepped in to fill necessary roles and jobs in the absence of men gained a greater sense of self-worth and a desire to move outside the traditional roles of homemaker and mother. Consumer goods that were never imagined or accessible were now within easy reach, and the technology that was so much a part of the war effort became an integral part of day-to-day life, changing the norm forever.

Edmonton's economy has grown significantly during the war years. For example, construction activity rose to $7,988,348 in 1945 from $1,661,109 in 1939. The Edmonton that greeted the troops returning from World War II differed from the city to which World War I veterans returned. This time troops did not have to confront the consequences of an influenza epidemic or the seeds of the Depression. Instead, the Edmonton of 1945 was a growing city with many opportunities despite the risks.

⌇ ⌇

During this era of turmoil and transition, the EFCL increased its civic participation and actively continued its effort to improve the quality of life across the city. As early as 1930, the EFCL and its leagues were a well-recognized voice on social and community-related issues. For example, on April 18, 1930, the *Edmonton Bulletin* reported that the Eastwood Community League had asked for a reduction of the mill rate, the establishment of a sidewalk, and protection from speeding cars in its area. Mayor Douglas reportedly instructed the police chief to station a motorcycle officer every evening at the offending intersection to seize the speeders. On June 5 of that year, the *Bulletin* again reported a protest by the EFCL, this time against a filling station that the EFCL deemed to be hazardous to life and limb.

In November, the EFCL was again in the news, this time about the increasing crime rate. At its annual general meeting, held in the public library on November 13, much of the discussion focused on the crime wave and the distribution of police resources. League representatives believed that the allocation of constables was ineffective because an insufficient number served on patrol duties. The EFCL resolved to establish a committee that would watch over the activities and organization of the Edmonton Police Department. A resolution urged city council to conduct an "immediate official investigation of the force."

Health services and accessibility dominated the agenda at the EFCL regular meeting on January 13, 1931. The issue was provincial government funding of fifty cents per day for each Isolation Hospital patient. Health and hospital officials deemed the funding insufficient for the hospital to maintain its patients. The city was recruited to help, but was unsuccessful in its effort to increase provincial funding and sought to establish the equivalent of user fees. This brought the EFCL into the discussion. It invited the medical superintendent of the Royal Alexandra and the Isolation hospitals, Dr. A. F. Anderson, and alderman D. K. Knott, who was also a member of the hospital board, to discuss the matter. According to the *Bulletin*, one of the options discussed (and discarded) was that wage earners should contribute a small amount each month from their paycheque toward the maintenance of the hospital service. The other opinion was to press the province to "be responsible for 50% of the Isolation Hospital deficit," which became the EFCL position.

The EFCL attracted countless of volunteers from all walks of life. Many brought life experiences that had proved successful elsewhere. One such volunteer was Dorothy (Dott) Adair (nee Trembley).

Born in Purcell, Oklahoma, in 1887, Dott immigrated with her family to Canada in 1901 and settled in South Edmonton. After graduating from Edmonton's only high school, she began work at the *Edmonton Bulletin*, and there she met her future husband, Joseph Woods Adair, who would serve two terms as alderman (1921–24) and as deputy mayor. Even before her marriage in 1921, the future Mrs. Adair was actively involved in local affairs, often promoting women's rights even before Emily Murphy (who lived three houses over from her in the Garneau area) gained recognition. In 1921, when the oldest of her four children started school, Adair became active in the Garneau Parent Teacher Association, which evolved into the Garneau Community League.

For the next thirty years, Adair continued to work tirelessly for her league. She was the first woman to be elected league president, and the first woman to join the EFCL board. Adair was also a founding member of the Cooperative Commonwealth Federation (CCF) Party in Alberta and chair of the War Savings Stamps Committee for Edmonton during World War II. She was also on the executive of the Women's Institute, the Granite Curling Club, the Garneau Bowling Club, the Alberta Ladies' Curling Association, and the Alberta Ladies' Lawn Bowling Association.

Dott and Joe Adair both died in 1960. On September 13, 2003, the city dedicated a park in the Garneau Community League area in their honour.

During the sixteen months following the crash of the New York Stock Exchange, the issues dealt by the EFCL included increased crime, health care, and increased taxation through user fees. Yet when the EFCL held its annual banquet on February 26, 1931, in the new Riverdale community hall, the mood was optimistic and upbeat. The gala event drew nearly 200 guests, including Lieutenant Governor William Egbert, Attorney General John F. Lymburn, Mayor J. M. Douglas and his Deputy Rice Sheppard, representatives of the school board, and numerous other dignitaries. Their speeches, reported in the February 28 issue of the Bulletin, only briefly mentioned the difficulties confronted by government. Canon C. F. A. Clough, in a toast to the city and a brief address, painted the city's future in glowing colours, predicting that Edmonton would expand along with the growth of the North to which the city was gateway. Deputy Mayor Sheppard responded to the toast and noted that the current depressed conditions reflected a worldwide situation. He added that with patience and cooperation things would come back to normal. An interesting sidebar was a brief speech made by Dr. F. Crang about educational matters. He advocated the creation of regional high schools in each of the separate districts across the city instead of a single central facility, observing that this reflected the wishes of the public.

Civic politics continued to be a topic of discussion. On March 13, the Bulletin again reported on the EFCL's regular meeting, held the night before in council chambers, where two EFCL candidates were elected to the advisory council to the school board. League representatives observed that the EFCL was under-represented on that advisory council and passed a motion directing EFCL president E. E. Howard to request four positions on the council.

By April, the escalating Depression and its economic and social consequences finally got the leagues' full attention. At the EFCL's April 16 meeting, the leagues passed a resolution "that the question of the economic depression be the subject of debate and general discussion at the next regular meeting of the federation." In the meantime, the EFCL continued to advance the cause of sports and recreation in Edmonton. In April, it established new leagues for soccer and softball, with the teams representing the various community leagues.

As financial woes were becoming more and more common, the EFCL continued to fight on the side of fiscal restraint, especially regarding fee or tax increases. On May 10, the Bulletin reported that a day earlier the EFCL had unanimously passed a motion opposing any increase to the water rate. This followed the city's installation of a water-softening plant, at an estimated cost of $86,300, which would have resulted in a 15-percent increase in the utility fees to its customers.

A month later, the EFCL was again in the news. This time its concern was library hours, which seemed inadequate given the needs of patrons. The EFCL board was also concerned about the closure of fire station No. 1 and the apparent centralization of firefighting resources at the 104th Street fire station. Fire chief Albert Dutton attended the meeting and defended his actions. He noted that he was not in favour of centralization and preferred to have stations throughout the area for faster response. He added that with the mechanization of the fire trucks, the fire department could quickly respond to any part of the city. By way of example, he said, "This week a call from Fort Saskatchewan was answered in thirty minutes."

While preoccupied with a myriad other issues, the EFCL nevertheless spent much attention on the worsening financial conditions. To be sure, life went on, but conditions were tough, with unemployment seen as the greatest issue at hand. To mediate the consequences of unemployment, the EFCL began to agitate for the "conscription of wealth" (EFCL minutes, June 11, 1931). After lengthy debate during its June 11 meeting, the EFCL passed a resolution in support of unemployment insurance, which it presented a few days later at a citizens' conference on the issue of unemployment. Another resolution from that meeting encouraged the various governments to immediately undertake a make-work project involving the construction of a national highway.

While much discussion focused on the plight of the unemployed, the meeting's agenda covered a number of other topics. Most notable among them, especially in the view of the Edmonton Journal (June 12, 1931), was the debate about coeducation in Edmonton's high schools. Some denounced the practice as "disgraceful," "infernal," and "abominable." In the end, however, the chair, President E. Howard, deftly deferred the topic to another meeting.

By September, the financial depression and its impact on the local economy had become a regular and prominent issue on the EFCL agenda. The Citizens' Relief Committee—a loose coalition of community agencies—approached the EFCL to use its league network to investigate existing needs within the community, identify the needy, and collect relief resources for them. After much debate, which included divergent views regarding the problem and its solution, the EFCL finally voted unanimously to serve as the investigative arm of the relief committee.

The October 15 meeting, held at its usual venue, the council chamber, again involved controversy. One of the key topics of discussion was whether a woman who was married to an employed man should be released to allow an unemployed man the opportunity to work. A resolution passed unanimously, protesting to city council and all large businesses in town the continued employment of married women who were the second wage-earner in their family.

The meeting's agenda included a number of other hot topics. The federation appointed two delegates to appear before the school board and protest the increase in rental fees charged to community leagues for the use of school facilities. It also delegated its secretary to contact the public library to request it stay open longer hours during the winter months. In addition, a lengthy discussion followed a presentation by the town-planning expert, J. F. D. Tanqueray, on the current and future direction of street development. He spoke about the need to have main arteries and side streets. This approach allowed for a framework of key transportation routes, with side streets providing access to residential or commercial properties. (It established the current system.) At the end, despite objections by some leagues, the EFCL supported "the principle of the plan as a benefit to Edmonton in the years to come" (*Edmonton Journal*, October 16, 1931).

While active on its concerns regarding public welfare and adequate infrastructure, the EFCL continued its efforts to expand its recreational programs. In 1931, it established a sports committee that quickly set out to form subcommittees, each providing for a separate sport: football, swimming, and diving. The committee also held an annual horseshoe-pitching competition, with its own trophy.

A review of the *Edmonton Journal* coverage of 1932 reflects an extensive effort by the EFCL and its leagues to conduct fundraising activities at every possible opportunity. Countless whist drives and social events raised funds for league programs and the needy, while the EFCL continued its aggressive lobbying on community-related issues. One such matter was the extension of the city's waterworks infrastructure to the municipality of Spruce Grove, west of Edmonton. The opposition, which prevented the extension of the infrastructure, argued the higher need by existing and new leagues for that service. In fact, many of the leagues were working within the federation to pursue city council for basic infrastructure and services.

One such case was the Calgary Trail Community League, which petitioned the city for a bus route to replace the existing streetcar service. A plebiscite during the previous municipal election had defeated a motion to replace the McKernan Lake streetcar line with a bus route. However, the league argued that the ballot form was confusing and that many people were misled by information handed to them as they entered the polling booth. This controversy and a number of other planning-related issues had prompted the EFCL, in April of that year, to wade once again into city planning. Some outside the EFCL assumed that, once the city accepted the report on the city's street planning, the task of the city planner and his committee was over. The EFCL took the stand that the task of planning had just begun. Despite the costs of the city planning department, reported by the *Edmonton Journal* (April 15, 1931) at $3,300, the EFCL unanimously support the continuation of the city's planning department.

Another major controversy related to the summer fair. The federation debated the continuation of the fair and voted to support it, with the condition that gambling at the fair be terminated and overall costs reduced. This stance was based on a study conducted by the ex-mayor, J. M. Douglas, which illustrated that those who spent (and lost) their money at the fair were the ones least likely to be able to afford the loss.

The next major controversy to hit the EFCL occurred in April 1932 and related to sports activities on Sundays. With the growing interest in sports, more and more participants in increasing number of sports had been keeping EFCL organizers busy. The EFCL had also established organizing committees for swimming, soccer, softball, and hardball to coordinate and facilitate these sports at the local level. In short, more and more sports activities (including competitions) were demanding more and more attention, space, and scheduling time.

The matter was brought to a head when the federation's wildly successful and fast-growing sports programs (especially hockey and basketball) left no playtime available other than on Sundays. Federation Secretary W. C. Deane initiated the discussion by noting that the intent was not to make Sunday hockey playing a norm. He noted that the proposed change of EFCL policy would avoid a repetition of a situation that had occurred a few months earlier when two games had to be played on the same evening to meet game-schedule needs without playing on Sunday. Federation President Ben Hager favoured allowing Sunday hockey games, as did representatives of the Walterdale Community League. However, some federation executives (including past president E. E. Howard) and representatives of the Cromdale Community League were against the proposal. A fierce debate ensued, with those opposing calling the proposed change the "thin edge of the wedge," inferring that it would result in more sport competitions on the Sabbath (*Edmonton Journal*, April 14, 1931). Speaking in favour of the proposal, Hager was quoted in the *Journal* as saying: "We are a non-sectarian organization and should remain as such." The federation voted to defer the matter until the leagues had time to deliberate on their position. At the end, when the matter of Sunday sports finally came to a vote by the leagues, the decision was in favour of changing the old and restrictive policy.

Meanwhile, community life continued, with sports, recreation, and community infrastructure a concern. When the sewer system was damaged by mining activities, the Riverdale Community League teamed up with the Riverdale Property Owner's Association to lobby the city for a better sewer system. Citing health risks and the potential for epidemics, they demanded immediate action. The two community leagues of Jasper Place and Westgrove were both seeking to establish community halls.

Other areas of interest for the community leagues involved the annual "Clean-up Drive," plans for the zoo at Borden Park, an overhead bridge at 109th Street, a plan to reduce the interest rate on money lent by the city to leagues, the state of education in the city, and negotiation on amusement tax. The latter involved the EFCL in negotiations with the provincial government and the organizers of the speed skating carnival to reduce the tax levied on such events involving the community leagues.

By early 1934, the federation included twenty-one leagues. This reflected the growing reputation and strength of the community league movement as well as the city's swelling population. The increase in EFCL membership was not without its growing pains, perhaps due to the financial pressures of the times or the strain of demands on volunteers. Nevertheless, some community leagues— Glenora, Central, and Norwood-Patricia—temporarily became defunct, and the EFCL assumed responsibility for their operations. Similarly, the Calgary Trail Community League resigned from the federation, re-entering it a short time

Land shift in the Riverdale
community area due to
coal mining, 1927.
City of Edmonton Archives
EA 10-1429.

later as a newly organized league. Given the reorganization of some of its league members, the EFCL approved boundary extensions for leagues that wanted them, as long as the new boundary did not involve existing leagues or those under reorganization.

As if that was not enough, the EFCL had to resolve a dispute in Forest Heights Community League regarding which of two individuals was the legal president. EFCL President Ben Hager settled the matter amicably, resulting in Mr. C. Overall's reaffirmation as the league's president.

For the EFCL, politics was not restricted to the organization's internal operations. Its reach went beyond Edmonton's elected officials and municipal administration to include provincial and federal officials. For example, the president of the Highland Community League, J. A. Ross, was able to interview Prime Minister R. B. Bennett, who was passing through Edmonton en route to Ottawa, and discuss with him the need to reduce the interest rate charged on municipal bonds. According to the Edmonton Journal (January 12, 1934), Mr. Bennett promised to "give serious consideration to the matter of ... building of a vehicle and pedestrian deck on the CNR bridge at Clover Bar."

Although the relationship between the EFCL and city administration appeared to be based on cooperation, it had its moments of conflict and disagreement. Occasionally, issues forced the EFCL to take a stand against city policies or practices. One such situation related to the cost of riding the local streetcars. The rates (reported by the *Edmonton Journal* on March 9, 1934) were ten cents per ticket, twenty-five cents for booklets of four tickets, or one dollar for twenty tickets. The city privatized the sale of these tickets and made them available through department stores across Edmonton. The EFCL objected to the process on two grounds. It argued that the cost distribution discriminated against the poor, who could not afford to pay the one-dollar cost to gain the lowest individual cost per ticket. Moreover, while some department stores began to sell the five-cent tickets separately, that still forced the poor to go to these stores and purchase the tickets.

The federation also demanded the creation of gravelled streets, sidewalks, and playgrounds across Edmonton. It sought changes to the sanitary laws, which appeared to force residents to connect their homes to the sanitary system that was not readily available, while a number of municipal facilities near a sanitary system remained disconnected. The federation also discussed tax exemption for league-operated refreshment stands connected to the league's rink. The discussion included the potential loss of business opportunity to local businesses. The counter view noted that the money raised through these stands was not in competition with established businesses, but was for community league operations that benefited all residents. The debate concluded with the passing of a resolution directing the EFCL to lobby the municipality and the province for an exemption from the tax. Less than a month later, the city finance committee did exempt the league-operated refreshment booths from taxes.

Not all EFCL-city interactions were confrontational or on matters of the local infrastructure. In February 1935, the EFCL went to bat in support of Mayor Clarke. The issue was over day and night shifts at the street railway department. It seemed that the more senior employees had an apparent monopoly over the day shifts, while junior employees were assigned many years of ongoing night shifts. The dispute involved a disagreement between the All-Canadian Union and the International Trade Union, which preferred the status quo for its more senior members. In the end, the EFCL supported a more balanced approach to the allocation of both day and night shifts.

Nevertheless, cooperation with the mayor was short-lived and was again put to the test over his push for a stadium. The issue was not over Edmonton's need for a stadium; rather, it exploded over the use of federal funds. Mayor Clarke, a veteran of the Klondike Gold Rush expedition and an avid athlete, wanted to use $50,000 from a federal relief grant of $500,000. The EFCL argued that the federal grant was for job creation and should be allocated strictly for that purpose. According to the Edmonton Journal (April 12, 1935), some delegates to the April meeting of the EFCL felt that Edmonton "needs road construction and maintenance more than it needs a stadium."

During the April meeting, EFCL President Lloyd Jones suggested that the federal government should be lobbied to pay municipal taxes on its city properties. The league delegates at the meeting quickly put the matter to rest based on the impact of the federal presence on local employment and other such services. They also noted that any effort to tax these buildings might result in the diversion of future capital projects to other cities. The issue received no further attention without any apparent damage to Jones's reputation. In November of that year, the membership unanimously elected him for a second term as president. In November 1939, Jones started his sixth consecutive term as president.

As time went on, the federation continued its involvement with sports and recreational programs, as well as with other local issues. Some of these issues involved support of the opening of the Edmonton power station on a full-time basis, extension of the bus route to include Forest Heights, creation of an inter-league debating competition, reduction of overcrowding in elementary schools, and construction of the cenotaph at an estimated cost of $10,000. The cenotaph, which was unveiled in 1936, was particularly poignant, given the unfolding of events that led to World War II.

In late 1938, the EFCL had twenty-three member leagues with a combined membership of 10,000 people. It had been very active in local issues and very vocal on many of the local political issues. On September 2, the Edmonton Journal reported that the EFCL was selecting candidates for the upcoming annual civic elections—reportedly due to the EFCL's dissatisfaction with the treatment of its league members by civic politicians and administration. The EFCL accused current and past members of city council of focusing inappropriately on the internal politics of their administration instead of focusing on the needs of the public.

Lloyd Jones, the EFCL president, also objected to the current system of administration and argued in favour of a ward system based on the existing community league boundaries. He was quoted in the *Journal* (September 24) saying that

> Community leagues serve as a training ground, which would be of value in the administration of the city's affairs.... There are men interested in the leagues in the various parts of the city who have a better civic background and a better civic consciousness than have many members of the present civic council. These men have an intimate understanding of the conditions that exist in their immediate localities and in many cases know more of what is actually going on in their city than the city fathers.

The matter persisted, and in January of the following year, the EFCL voted to make its civic affairs committee a permanent part of its organization. On January 19, the *Edmonton Journal* quoted the current chair of the civic committee, Elisha East, who said, "It is of utmost importance that the members of our community leagues understand all public utilities and to create a public opinion on civic affairs." Grant McConachie, the famous bush pilot and prominent business executive, and another league member supported East. McConachie suggested that the committee should "protest the action of the city in granting permits for indiscriminate building of houses in the twenty-mill zone so that the owners can evade higher taxes closer to the city centre."

Following the declaration of war, the EFCL joined others in the debate about how to fund the war. The EFCL discussed a motion recommending that the federal government should first conscript wealth before conscripting the youth of the nation. The federation deferred the matter to the community leagues for discussion at their regular meetings. The EFCL also approved financial support for league-operated ice rinks and forwarded its recommendation to the city.

In early November, at the EFCL's annual general meeting, the membership elected Lloyd Jones to his fifth consecutive term as president and easily reinstated W. C. Deane to his fifteenth term as secretary. A number of the reports outlined the growth of the federation and its achievements. Grant McConachie, the chairman of the civic committee (and a school board trustee), discussed his committee's effort to reduce the price of milk given to students. The price was eventually reduced to two cents per pint. Lloyd Wood, the federation representative on the Royal Alexandra Hospital Board (and its chair), highlighted the board's many achievements. These included the purchase of special and costly ($15,000) equipment that according to the *Journal* "will cure 35% of cancer cases. [It was] the only therapy machine of its kind in western Canada."

A month later, the EFCL was back in the news with its concern for the well-being of league residents. It demanded that the city establish utilities, sidewalks, and other community league-level improvements. It approached the province, in support of the city, to request a reduction in natural gas rates for the city's residents. It also approached the committee that organized the June 2 visit to Edmonton by their majesties King George VI and Queen Elizabeth for disbursement of its revenue funds. The EFCL had incurred a debt of $300, which it wanted reduced.

The federation and its member leagues continued to be active in fundraising activities (notably dances and whist drives) and recreational programs including the summer and winter carnivals. These were major and well-attended events, but they were not the federation's only focus. When Mayor John Fry opened the eighth EFCL Winter Carnival, the federation was again active in a network of agencies established to assist the population through the hardship of war. Lloyd Jones and EFCL Secretary James Miller became delegates to the Edmonton Council of Social Agencies.

The second summer carnival was held in July 1940 at a location north of Jasper Avenue and 102nd Street, attracting an estimated crowd of 3,000 on its opening evening. This was an important event for the leagues, because the proceeds from the carnival were for Edmonton's fund for the welcome of evacuee children from the "Old Country"—England. Shortly afterward, in September, the federation took the extra step to directly support the war effort. It voted unanimously to support the city's "Spitfire Fund," which was to fund the purchase of a Spitfire fighter for the war effort. In December, the EFCL voted to support a recent ban by the city's fruit merchants of Japanese mandarin oranges for the duration of the war.

The effort in support of the war was not restricted to the federation. One by one, the leagues began to take independent action to support their own *cause célèbre*. The Rossdale community held a skating party to raise funds for the Greek

war relief, the Calder community held a New Year's party to raise funds for the Canadian Red Cross, the McCauley community held concerts to promote the sale of war saving stamps, and the Riverdale community held a concert to fund children evacuated from England.

As the war in Europe accelerated in pace and intensity, Mayor Fry approached the federal government with a request to establish more war-related industries in the city. His request was supported by an EFCL resolution that encouraged the development of such industries within Edmonton. The EFCL, which was a member of a task force to review rent increases in the city, also passed (in March 1941) a resolution requesting that the city lobby to be included in the federal government's rent control program. At the same time, the federation cabled a donation of one hundred dollars to G. W. Wilkinson, the lord mayor of London, as a contribution to a fund for children evacuated to other parts of the British Empire. In time, other such donations continued, with thanks received directly from the lord mayor.

Municipal politics returned to the EFCL agenda in September 1941, when the federation opposed the city's scheme to sell water to Spruce Grove, located west of Edmonton. Spruce Grove residents received their water from a private contractor that hauled the water in special tankers; Edmonton proposed selling water directly to that municipality, which would then distribute it through its own system.

A month later, at its annual general meeting, the EFCL went through another change of personnel. Its president, J. J. Hodgkinson, had resigned in May to devote more time to the Queen's Canadian Fund for air-raid victims, and Vice-President J. B. Gilles had taken over the vacated presidency role. For the previous eight years, Gilles was also president of the Westmount Community League. He thus brought to the federation post a sense of reality at league level. He also assumed responsibility for a federation that was growing in numbers as well as involvement. EFCL activities included representation on the city library board, the Royal Alexandra Hospital board, the Edmonton Exhibition board, and the Consumers' League. It operated with an increasing number of committees: civic, carnival, dramatics, handicrafts, publicity, and social.

Naturally, the federation's involvement in these committees was in addition to its involvement in various sports programs, which were demanding in and of themselves. For example, the 1940–41 hockey program involved 234 boys playing in eighteen teams and three divisions—midget, juveniles, and juniors. The program's motto was "Give every boy a chance to play," and its success and continued growth spoke for itself. It operated at a cost of $1,170.

During its December 1941 meeting, the EFCL went head to head with the Edmonton Exhibition over the intended continuation of the latter's midway and race meet, scheduled for the summer period. The federation complained about the reversal of a decision, made a year earlier by the Exhibition, to discontinue the races. They waged a fierce debate, with those opposing the races wanting to minimize, as much as possible, the wastage of money that might otherwise be available to enhance the war effort. Others noted that neither the United Kingdom nor Australia, both closer to the war effort than Canada, had abandoned horseracing. The final vote was sixteen to six in favour of delivering a statement of protest to the city regarding the intended continuation of the raceway.

Another equally controversial item on the EFCL agenda was its opposition to the extension of the retirement age for city employees. EFCL past president Lloyd Jones noted that many city employees aged fifty to fifty-five were prevented from advancement because the city was keeping older men past their retirement age. His motion to oppose this practice won support despite a few dissenting votes. The members agreed that the city should be encouraged to retire those who had reached retirement age, unless they were indispensable in their jobs.

Another topic on the agenda involved a demand by various leagues, supported by the EFCL, to increase the police force. Discussion around a motion for more streetlights reached no conclusion or commitment for action by the EFCL. Another hotly discussed issue was the matter of providing free after-school skating in return for the grants provided by the public and separate school boards. League delegates at the meeting agreed on the urgent requirement for free skating time, but argued that the sum of the grant (estimated at $8.30 per rink) did not allow for the expected operation of the rinks.

Discussion at the EFCL's March 1942 meeting focused on the war effort close to home related to blackout drills across Edmonton. Representatives of the Corps of Imperial Frontiersmen and of the St. John Ambulance were at hand to drive home the need for more training and greater attention to the blackout drills. They noted that, under current conditions, each auxiliary police officer in Edmonton had to cover an area of about sixty blocks within the five-minute warning time. He had to rush around and blow his whistle, thereby alerting area residents to mask the light coming from their home or place of business. This approach was obviously not working, and the two organizations were approaching the EFCL for help. They wanted it to encourage its member leagues and their residents to attend training sessions held weekly at the police station and to appoint a first aid coordinator for each community league. St. John Ambulance agreed to train and coordinate league volunteers. Shortly thereafter, Edmonton saw the installation of many air-raid sirens in public facilities, including community halls. (Edmonton decommissioned the last air-raid siren in service in early 1990.)

A month later, the federation seemed to be involved in a single issue—streetcar fares. The city had proposed to raise the price of a book of tickets. The federation representatives objected strenuously because it was felt that the street railway system was trying to eliminate its deficit on the back of riders. The only resolution at the meeting was to demand that the city leave the streetcar fares unchanged. The discussion also addressed rising meat prices, but without reso-lution. Instead, the federation accepted a suggestion from Riverdale league repre-sentative Ben Hager to let the Edmonton Consumers' League investigate the matter.

Hager also suggested that the federation develop closer ties with the Consumers' League. Half a year later, the closer working relationship became a reality when the two organizations decided to place a representative on each other's board and work together on issues of mutual concern. One such concern, raised in November 1942, was that the cost of milk seemed high and was likely to rise. Guided by the Consumers' League, the federation lobbied for an increase in the catchment areas for dairy farmers from the current 25-kilometre (15-mile) radius to 80 kilometres (50 miles). This change was to increase the number of dairy farmers allowed to sell their milk to the city's residents. The two organizations also argued that Edmonton residents should have the choice of having milk delivered to their house or buying it from a store. That process was expected to reduce the cost of the milk.

The city's electoral system was again an item of discussion by the EFCL. The chairman of its publicity committee, Ben Hager, went on record to condemn the current system of electing aldermen at large, which did not assign them responsibility for a particular geographic area or its residents. Hager argued that many parts of the city—McCauley, Calder, Westmount, North Edmonton, East Strathcona, Riverdale, Rossdale, Cloverdale, and Calgary Trail—had no real representation because they had no one specific to address their needs. He advocated the ward system, which he described as working in other Canadian cities such as Toronto, Winnipeg, Windsor, and Montreal. The federation accepted his suggestion and forwarded it to the city. In April 1944, after having received no response, the federation pressed the city to hold a plebiscite on the matter at the next civic election in November of that year.

Another issue—the dumping of ashes from fireplaces and the like—was raised as a health concern, triggered by the spreading of ashes, often laden with nails or broken glass, on streets and alleyways across the city. The ashes were presenting a terrible smell as well. A motion by J. P. Morris committed the federation to asking city council to check on regulations to ensure curtailment of the practice.

By 1944, the war in Europe was progressing well, and a number of organizations, including the federation, began to focus on post-war reconstruction. One component of the reconstruction was education—reminiscent of the post-World War I period, when returning veterans had flooded educational institutions in their quest to make up for lost time and missed opportunity.

The superintendent of schools, R. S. Sheppard, approached the EFCL for support in the construction of a high school that would meet the needs of children and adults. The proposed school was to be an extension of Victoria High School and provide a wide array of academic, commercial, and technical programs. It was to be a massive undertaking involving two gymnasiums, an auditorium, indoor pool, tennis courts, a cafeteria, and separate fields for soccer, softball, and rugby. The EFCL approved the development of such a school, which in time became a reality.

The federation expected the post-war period, like the 1919 era, to bring a significant increase in the demand for recreation and sports from returning veterans. In early 1945, the EFCL began discussions about the construction of a park to replace what seemed to be an eyesore, in the area next to the Hotel Macdonald. The matter was deferred to the leagues with a statement from EFCL president Percy Cowley (reported in the *Journal* on January 12) noting: "If any money is spent by the city it should be on housing. Too many people are living in hovels and even tents."

While the park issue was deferred, the matter of playgrounds and fields was hotly debated through much of the year. The city's recreation commission had proposed a five-year plan, starting in 1946, to establish five fully equipped recreational centres in the city. The EFCL countered with a suggestion that the recreation commission level off the area around each league's playground and turn it into playing fields. The EFCL argued that its proposal would extend the capacity of the sports programs to meet increasing demands.

As in previous years, the EFCL continued to spend much time organizing its softball, soccer, basketball, figure skating, hockey, and speed skating programs. The last two were particularly active. Interest in boxing also grew and organizers proposed that, if each league developed its own facility, they would have no difficulty recruiting coaches and trainers. However, the proposal went no further.

At the conclusion of World War II, the EFCL anticipated the return of veterans to the city and began to look at its future. On numerous occasions, mostly during its major anniversaries, the EFCL had looked back in time and marvelled at its achievements. In late 1945, the federation stood at a major crossroad, wondering about its future. During its November meeting W. S. Baldwin, president of the Cloverdale League, recounted the outcome of a recent meeting involving eighteen community league presidents. They met to discuss the EFCL governance and future operations, and concluded that the EFCL needed to incorporate under the 1924 Societies Act of Alberta. They discussed and then deferred the matter to the February 1946 general meeting with words of encouragement from EFCL President Kenneth Lewis, who supported incorporation.

On November 9, the *Edmonton Journal* quoted Baldwin, who "stressed the urgent necessity that the federation become solidified under the act to enable [it] to go forward more strongly and energetically with a legal status, in the endeavour to promote goodwill, recreation, education, and social intercourse on a more solid foundation." It was a vision that time proved correct.

Each of us makes a difference.
It is from numberless acts of courage
and belief that human history is shaped.

— ROBERT F. KENNEDY

4

Black Gold, Roughnecks, and a Booming Community

1947–1960

Exceed expectations.
We are not driven to do extraordinary things,
but to do ordinary things extraordinarily well.
— BISHOP GORE

FOUGHT TO OVERCOME ONE MENACE, World War II ended with the world splintered along east–west lines to confront another menace. The Cold War was soon a reality. The military threat posed by Russia's armament and its acquisition in 1949 of the nuclear bomb, plus the experience of the Korean War (1950–53), created a growing demand for oil and minerals such as iron, aluminium, and uranium. These were necessary for increasing military preparedness in North America and elsewhere. Oil replaced coal, which until then had sustained much of the economy but now seemed insufficient.

Edmonton and Alberta, which relied heavily on coal, suddenly found their wealth diminished and their opportunities reduced.[1] For both, the future, especially in the immediate post-war era, was less promising than anticipated. Part of the problem was that, despite Edmonton's fast growth and frantic war-related activity, it had invested little effort or resources in enhancing its infrastructure. For example, during the ten years prior to 1945, the length of Edmonton's paved roads increased by only 19 kilometres (12 miles) and its sidewalks by 51 kilometres (32 miles). With nearly 40 percent built before 1920, Edmonton homes reflected the city's aging infrastructure. Mayor Harry Ainlay and the

Imperial Oil's Leduc No. 1
oil well goes into production,
February 13, 1947.
Provincial Archives of Alberta,
J.312/2, PA P2729.

Edmonton Chamber of Commerce tried valiantly to attract new industries, but had to cope with the reality of the sharp decline of the previously dominant coal industry. Edmonton's other main industry, farming, was slowly increasing production; however, the number of farmers began a permanent and steady decline.

The demand for fuel rose significantly due to the increasing number of vehicles that ploughed across Alberta's roadways and to the growing industrial base that demanded an alternate fuel source to coal: oil! Unfortunately, the Turner Valley oil field was running dry, and local oil refineries had to import oil from the United States. By mid-February 1947, all of that changed forever, and with it the future of Edmonton and Alberta.

On February 13, 1947, Alberta, and to a lesser degree Edmonton, hit a jackpot: Leduc Oil Well No. 1. By 1954 the site, owned by Imperial Oil and only 27 kilometres (17 miles) southwest of Edmonton's post office (a key city landmark) turned out to be a collection of 1,278 producing oil wells that contained an estimated 200 million barrels of crude oil. The discovery spurred Imperial Oil and other oil companies to accelerate their exploration activities in the area around Edmonton. One by one, these companies discovered and developed new fields and added new names to their success list. They included the Woodbend field operated by Imperial Oil 23 kilometres (14 miles) west of Edmonton's post office, the nearby Leduc-Woodbend field operated by the Canadian Atlantic Oil Company, the Redwater field located 50 kilometres (30 miles) northeast of Edmonton, the Pembina field located 140 kilometres (85 miles) southwest of Edmonton, and the Joarcam field 40 kilometres (25 miles) outside of Edmonton. The oil companies discovered many other fields around Stettler, Big Valley, Bon Accord, Calmar, Wizard Lake, and elsewhere, all within 80 kilometres (50 miles) of Edmonton.

Drilling activity in the area grew rapidly. From 1947 to 1956, the number of existing wells increased from 418 to 7,390. Production too increased dramatically, from 1.4 billion cubic metres (50 billion cu. ft.) in 1946 to four times as much by 1956. It was but the tip of the horn of plenty.

The discovery of producing oil wells in the area spurred tremendous development beyond anything imagined. In the decade ending in 1956, the petroleum industry $2.5 billion into the Alberta economy. In the Clover Bar area alone, the industry invested over $400 million in new manufacturing plants. The Sherritt Gordon plant, built in Fort Saskatchewan, cost over $60 million. The Celanese Canada chemical plant, one of the first of such plants in Edmonton, cost $40 million and took three years to build. Other plants were built by British American, McCall-Frontenac, Canadian Industries Limited (CIL), and Borden Chemicals.

The increased industrial activity in the petrochemical industry brought increased activity in other key sectors of the economy, notably the public sector and the University of Alberta. This in turn increased the demand for building and infrastructure construction. The city's population, around 113,200 in 1946, exceeded 551,300 by 1982. The value of building permits, totalling $15 million in 1946, grew to $1.5 billion by 1981. The construction frenzy was such that structural materials such as steel beams and concrete became in short supply. It typically took over a year to deliver orders of steel, and when contractors switched to cement blocks these too became in short supply. This situation prompted the Canada Cement Company and Inland Cement Company to build plants just outside the city limits.

The discovery of producing oil and gas wells in Edmonton's backyard created a need to transport the newly acquired natural resource to refineries, processing plants, and other markets. New refineries appeared in Edmonton's east and south end. As well, a major push was on to construct a network of pipelines that would eventually carry gas and liquids to destinations right across North America. Interprovincial Pipeline Company (IPL) built the first pipeline to cross the Alberta border. It was completed in December 1950 and carried products through Winnipeg to American destinations 1,129 miles away.

Alberta was experiencing an oil boom that affected every facet of its economy and would alter the future of its residents beyond the turn of the millennium. In 1946, the average annual income for every man, woman, and child in Alberta was $666; ten years later, that figure had more than doubled to $1,539. Alberta's treasury had also increased its wealth during the period. In 1946, Alberta collected $45 million in taxes and had a debt of approximately $145 million. By comparison, by 1956 the province had collected over $250 million in taxes, eliminated its debt, and amassed a saving fund of $250 million! Unsurprisingly, Alberta and its two largest cities, Edmonton and Calgary, became a destination of choice for countless new residents.

Between 1946 and 1956, Alberta's population increased by 40 percent or 320,000 people to 1,123,000. Edmonton's population doubled during that period. Its 1956 population of over 254,800 residents made Edmonton the sixth largest city in Canada, and like Calgary, one of the fastest-growing cities. This population growth and the availability of greater disposable income generated a frantic escalation of residential construction. On June 12, 1948, the *Edmonton Journal* reported the construction of 4,040 houses, 35 apartment blocks, and 20 duplexes in Edmonton since the end of the war, a short period of three years. Predictably, residential space in Edmonton was becoming scarce, and the city began extensive land annexation. Initially, this was most evident on the west end of the city with New Glenora, West Glenora, West Grove, and Jasper Place. Soon annexation extended to areas south, north, and east of the city.

Increasing industrial and residential construction put tremendous pressure on Edmonton's limited and inferior pre-war road and sidewalk networks, and necessitated their expansion. From 1946 to 1956, the total length of all Edmonton's roadways increased from 640 kilometres (396 miles) to 1,370 kilometres (853 miles), while paved roads increased from 110 kilometres (70 miles) to 430 kilometres (266 miles). Similar growth occurred with cement-based sidewalks, which more than doubled from a total length of 460 kilometres

(287 miles) to 1,070 kilometres (666 miles). Water mains and sewers followed suit, and their networks were upgraded and expanded at hitherto unparalleled pace. The demand for electricity continued to outstrip production capacity, triggering the construction of new power-generation plants and the upgrading of existing ones. Telephone services too became a hot commodity that outstripped available resources and the capacity to connect future users to the growing network. It was common for Edmonton's residents to wait a whole year for a new phone connection.

Boom-time economy, plentiful job opportunities, increasing personal wealth, and a host of new technological gadgets and innovations made life in the late 1940s and the 1950s exciting and rapidly evolutionary.[2] Modern mass-marketing techniques and the arrival in 1954 of television to Edmonton added great changes to the local scene. Shopping centres, drive-in movie theatres, restaurants, and laundromats became more common and promised personal freedom as well as more leisure time.

When the Seven Seas Restaurant opened in July 1948 on Jasper Avenue between 105th and 106th streets, it was Edmonton's only licensed restaurant. It could accommodate 650 patrons and employed over 100 staff members. For many years, it was the largest restaurant in western Canada. Soon more and more eatery establishments appeared, catering to the growing demand of Edmonton's residents for diverse menus and freedom from preparing their own meals.

The war era had seen a great increase in the demand for cars, with a resultant growth in car dealerships, garages, and service stations across Edmonton. Soon Jasper Avenue and many other main streets in Edmonton were congested with trolley cars, cars, horse-drawn wagons, and pedestrians. To alleviate some of the chaos of people parking everywhere, in 1948 the city introduced 800 parking meters to the downtown area. By 1954, the number of meters had increased to 2,000—for good reason. The demand for private cars had escalated exponentially. A year later, on February 12, 1955, the first underground public parking garage in Canada opened in Edmonton, just east of the Hotel Macdonald.

With traffic and parking quickly becoming a problem in the downtown area, developers and business executives began looking at the suburbs for the placement of their shopping centres and retail businesses. On August 18, 1955,

Woodward's store on 102 Avenue, circa 1940.
City of Edmonton Archives EA 10-1803.

Edmonton opened its first shopping mall—the Westmount Shoppers' Park, at 111th Avenue and Groat Road. Constructed at a cost of nearly $5 million, the mall provided forty stores and a 3,000-car parking lot. Woodward's Westmount Food Floor, located at the mall's north end, provided shoppers with a number of new conveniences including the use of shopping carts, tills or cash registers, and self-serve meat packages. Prior to these innovations, shoppers had to carry a small wire basket on their arms, and patiently wait for the checkout girls to add their purchases on a small adding machine.

Many other changes made Edmonton an exciting place to live, work, and play. In 1947, for example, Edmonton became the first Canadian city to replace incandescent

In 1948, one of the largest car dealerships in Edmonton, Waterloo Motors (currently Waterloo Ford Lincoln), was established at 107th Street and Jasper Avenue. Eight years later, it sold 2,600 cars—thus outselling all other car dealers in North America.

streetlights with mercury vapour streetlights. The city tried these along Jasper Avenue with good results and, in 1956, decided to establish these lights across the city, including all of its new subdivisions. In doing so, Edmonton established a record for being the first city in the world to order a large quantity of these lights.

On October 10, 1941, the Edmonton Public Library, in cooperation with the Edmonton Radial Railway, established the world's first streetcar library. In 1951, when streetcars were no longer running in Edmonton, the service continued through two bookmobile buses. (In 1946, the Edmonton Radial Railway changed its name to the Edmonton Transportation System. A year later, it adopted its current name, the Edmonton Transit System.)

The ever-increasing demand for mass transit brought additional changes, leading to the opening in June 1949 of the Greyhound Bus Depot at 102nd Street and 102nd Avenue. Built at a cost of $500,000, the terminal served until 1981 all four of the bus lines operating in western Canada. Greyhound Lines, the oldest of these bus lines, started in 1914 using horse-drawn wagons. In 1922, sleek grey buses replaced these wagons and gave the company its name. In May 1929, the Greyhound Company inaugurated its twice-daily run between Edmonton and Calgary.

Another major innovation in local transportation was the replacement, on September 1, 1951, of the noisy streetcars that had been part of Edmonton since November 1908 with quieter trolley buses. During that time, Edmonton had the distinction of having the northernmost electric streetcars in North America. A few years later, in 1964, Edmonton became the first Canadian city to purchase Japanese-built buses.

The wave of prosperity had touched one facet after another of Edmonton, building confidence and generating greater prosperity. This confidence in Edmonton's success and potential led Edmonton in the mid-1950s to finally construct a city hall. On May 31, 1957, this city hall officially opened and became one among the first wave of major structures built in Edmonton after the war. Constructed at a cost of $3.5 million, the hall was the pride of the city and served as an extension of its golden anniversary celebration. Moreover, amid this celebration, one name stood out again and again—Mayor William Hawrelak.

After graduating from Victoria High School, Hawrelak worked on the family farm for a few years, returning to Edmonton in 1945 to become a multi-millionaire business executive and active community worker. He won his first mayoralty

Edmonton's Mayor Hawrelak
and his Council, 1955.
City of Edmonton Archives
EA 10-2612.

election in 1951, and continued a string of both victories and defeats until he died in office on November 7, 1975. Allegations of improprieties involving land transactions plagued his terms in office, and he twice lost his job as mayor. Yet he maintained tremendous popularity with Edmonton's residents, who voted him into the mayor's role for an unprecedented five terms. Part of Mayor Hawrelak's legacy was his push in the early 1950s for the development of Edmonton's international airport.

By 1956, Edmonton had secured its future within Alberta's growing wealth and fiscal confidence.[3]

With the experience of the Depression and the war behind it, the Edmonton Federation of Community Leagues (EFCL) found itself during the post-war era in a new *époque* and a very different operational environment. Yet one theme continued to be the main thread of its operations—the sustenance and enhancement of the quality of life for residents across the city.

On December 28, 1948, a group of local business executives formed the Edmonton Eskimo Rugby Football Club. In 1952, the club dropped the word rugby from its name. The club quickly made a name for itself by winning the 1954 Grey Cup championship, thanks to an incredible play by Jackie Parker, who recovered a fumble by the Montreal Alouette's Chuck Hunsinger with less than three minutes before the end of game to run a 95-yard touchdown.

The Edmonton Eskimos won the Grey Cup again in 1955, 1956, 1975, 1978, 1979, 1980, 1981, 1982, 1987, 1993, and 2003.

Recreation became a major issue, and the EFCL devoted much attention to ensuring its enhancement.[4] In 1945, the EFCL had assisted Alderman Harry Ainlay in forming the Edmonton Recreation Commission, tasked to look at the development of recreational facilities in the city. Based on the commission's recommendations, a special municipal department—the Municipal Parks Department—was formed in 1947 to play the lead role in developing and maintaining the city's recreational resources and programs. (The department was later renamed the Parks and Recreation Department, and more recently, the Community Services Department.) In the 1940s and 1950s, nearly a tenth of the city's area existed as park space.

At its January 1946 meeting, the EFCL asked the recreation commission to develop a strategy that would lead to the creation of community recreation centres. The EFCL also asked that the city spend all related budget appropriations for 1946 to clear and level ground within each league area for the development of league-operated sport fields. EFCL President Kenneth Lewis and the league presidents were adamant that the creation of sport fields (especially for leagues that did not have any) was the highest priority for the EFCL. The recreation commission chairman, Clarence Richards, and the city's supervisor of recreation, J. B. McGuire, agreed on the need to move quickly on this issue.

"We are way behind in recreational facilities at present ... [and] if we could agree to a plan, it would be a great help to all organizations," said Richards in the January 8 issue of the *Edmonton Journal*. The league presidents supported

Girls fastball finals, 1947.
City of Edmonton Archives EA 600-382A.

him, suggesting that if the city moved quickly to clear and level land for fields, the leagues would then have a basis to continue further development on their own.

While it supported recreation, the EFCL was careful to ensure that it kept an eye on other aspects relating to the quality of life in the city. As mentioned earlier, this became evident when the EFCL took a strong stand against a park across from the Hotel Macdonald, noting that its timing was poor, especially given the sorry state of housing in the city. Instead, the EFCL recommended that the funding for the park come from the Canadian National Railway, which owned the Hotel Macdonald and the land around it, instead of from Edmonton's taxpayers.

At around the same time, the EFCL committed to advancing its sports programs, most notably those involving skating, baseball, fastball, and soccer. After the federation agreed to provide instruction on "fancy skating" to community youngsters, past president Lloyd Jones was placed in charge of a committee to organize the lessons. Additionally, six new diamonds were constructed: two for baseball and four for fastball. Hardball and fastball leagues were established, the latter including intermediate men, juvenile boys, and

A sample of the parks constructed across Edmonton by the Gyro club.
City of Edmonton Archives EA 509-16.

midget and junior girls. To coordinate these and other activities, the EFCL also established three area conveners: Bill Kastings for the South Side, Jim Cowan for the East End, and Ed Orchin for the West End.

By May 1946, the federation was extremely active with its sports programs, and pushing the limits of possibility. In an attempt to raise $2,500 for its sports program, the EFCL created a flyer that highlighted its activities and promoted sports in the city. Approximately 1,500 businesses in the downtown area received the flyer, which requested that they contribute to the advancement of sports among the city's youth. A fifty-page booklet by Donald Cameron, head of the Department of Extension at the University of Alberta, complemented the flyer. Cameron relied on his twenty-year community-league experience across western Canada. The booklet, titled *Community Centres in Alberta*, described the benefits of community leagues and provided architectural drawings for the development of halls. This information, circulated across western Canada, assisted in many ways including the formation of Calgary's community leagues. By December, the EFCL began its sponsorship of a radio program called "Community League News" on CKUA, a leading local radio station.

With the renewed and increasing interest in recreation, the city's recreation commission approached the federation with a request that the leagues assume responsibility for the Gyro-operated playgrounds that the Gyro Club had turned over to the city. (Gyro was, and still is, an international social-focus agency.) The offer was accepted. The recreation commission also invited the leagues to send volunteers to a special course for instructors of "in-city" camps. Once qualified, these instructors conducted special summer camps for children of all ages in games, handicrafts, and other recreational activities. The city had operated such camps in 1944 and 1945; the leagues started to operate these camps in 1946 with assistance from the recreation commission. In addition to, or perhaps because of, this arrangement, the city agreed to the construction of seven new playgrounds— at Borden Park, Forest Heights, Bonnie Doon, Ritchie, Jasper Place, Cloverdale, and 101st Street at 120th Avenue—over a hectare (3 acres) of land and containing swings, slides, and teeter-totters. A. C. Patterson, the city's parks supervisor, provided each playground with trees to be planted by league volunteers.

By fall 1946, the EFCL realized that its capacity to deliver programs was significantly limited by its finances. After much deliberation, it decided to seek financial assistance from the Community Chest—the predecessor of the modern-day United Way. The federation successfully argued that it and its leagues were performing a community service comparable to that of the YMCA or other such organizations and were therefore entitled to financial assistance.

With each step, the federation was becoming more established and recognized for its community effort. This again became apparent during the October 1946 annual general meeting, when Ken Lewis was unanimously re-elected as president. At the same meeting Mayor Harry Ainlay was appointed honorary president (replacing the late A. E. Ottewell) and Johnny Caine, D.F.C. with two bars was elected to the board. (The bars signify more than one award of the same medal, the Distinguished Flying Cross.) Caine was Edmonton's most decorated World War II veteran and a resident of Parkallen. His election received wild applause from those in attendance. Other good news included the imminent increase in the number of community leagues and the incorporation of the EFCL as an Alberta society. Meeting attendees noted that both matters would enhance the federation's capacity to serve Edmonton residents.

An interesting story, reported by the Edmonton Journal on November 15, 1946, reveals the culture of the time and the spirit of the EFCL. W. H. Gimby, the

Forest Heights delegate to the EFCL general meeting, complained about the "scurrilous" literature to which Canadian children were exposed at newsstands. He complained that magazines were in poor English, featured crude or lurid stories, and contained a high number of advertisements for sex and alcohol. His solution did not involve prohibition or censorship. Instead, he argued strongly for an alternative option involving community centres for the whole family that would include shops, theatres, a library, and other forms of recreation, stating that these would serve as models for a healthier lifestyle.

"We must appeal to another emotion to replace the appeal of greed and sex underlined in the cheap magazine," he said. "The emotion that we, as a group of community workers, can appeal to is that of personal accomplishment and achievement." This was in line with the community league movement's strong belief in recreation and sport activities for youth as a foundation for a strong community.

In late January 1947, the EFCL suffered its first major loss when fire destroyed the Calder Community Hall. The two-storey building, located at 127th Avenue and 123rd Street, was one of the oldest in the district, dating back to 1912. Robert Dawson, a CNR switchman who along with his wife lived on the second floor above the community hall, had managed it. The fire gutted the building, and the Dawsons lost all of their belongings. The league president, Alberta A. Whiteman, was understandably upset about the loss of the hall and the irreplaceable league memorabilia, which included pictures of the winter and summer carnival queens, a collection of carnival costumes, and hockey equipment. However, as always, where the spirit is strong, no adversity leads to defeat.

By March, the community resolved to rebuild and began to hold dances to raise the necessary funds. By mid-August, the league secured a mortgage and acquired the former U.S. Army recreation hall, built during the war on the Jesuit College grounds. The 10-by-36-metre (36-by-120-foot) sheet metal structure, relocated to the Calder community playground area across from the Airport Hotel, immediately began to serve the community. (On October 8, 1952, the Edmonton Journal reported on the Calder mortgage-burning ceremony, attended by Mayor Hawrelak, EFCL President Charles Simmonds, and league president Percy Johnson.)

In February 1947, the EFCL and its leagues received a much-welcomed financial boost from city council. Until then, neither the city nor the local school

The EFCL-run Soap Box Derby, 1940.
City of Edmonton Archives EA 160-1457.

boards had matched the escalating operational costs for their ice rinks. Mayor Harry Ainlay and council decided to help relieve some of the resulting financial pressure on the leagues. They offered to pay the cost of the water used to flood league-operated ice rinks, as long as it did not exceed a total of two dollars per 93 square metres (1,000 square feet) of ice surface. The city also agreed to pay the cost of the electricity used to illuminate the rinks.

The increase in funding was good news for all the leagues, especially for the many with newly constructed or renovated ice rinks. For example, a year earlier Westmount had constructed a $12,000 skating rink, Central and Parkallen had opened their ice rink, and Cloverdale had carried out extensive repairs on its rink. Additionally, the leagues had constructed seven new playgrounds, and Ritchie had constructed its hall. By then, the EFCL's growing list of league members also included the Boyle Street League.

Community activities within the leagues and the EFCL continued to grow in both diversity and popularity. In September 1947, the EFCL again sponsored its annual soapbox derby, on McDougall Hill. According to the September 2 issue of the Edmonton Journal, the event drew more than 10,000 spectators. Later in the year, Charles Simmonds, a decorated war hero and past president of the McKernan District Community League, replaced Ken Lewis as EFCL president. By then, Windsor Community League and three newly established leagues had joined the EFCL, increasing its membership to thirty.

The EFCL continued its involvement in community issues. It recommended the establishment of blood donor clinics at the various community league halls, it established a new "welfare committee" to guide welfare work within each league, it expressed concerns about juvenile delinquency, and it spoke against the poor status of city planning. The federation raised the matter of city planning with city architect Max Dewar, who supported the idea of creating community centres where activities for all ages as well as business meetings could be conducted. He suggested that the city build these centres and that someone in city administration be responsible for neighbourhood planning. Of the two suggestions, the latter became a reality through the city, and the former came about through volunteers and their incredible fundraising efforts.

By April 1948, the EFCL and its leagues were again involved in a beautification project—the planting of trees throughout the city. This time, the project was in two phases. The first involved installing elm and ash trees, supplied free of charge by the city to leagues that agreed to supply the volunteer labour to plant them. City staff members guided these volunteers on the best method of planting these trees. Additionally, as part of an all-out war on mosquitoes, the city offered to supply a mixture of DDT and oil to all community league volunteers, who then were expected to spray pools of water within their community. Even the Edmonton Junior Chamber of Commerce got into the act and offered a subsidy to all community leagues that painted their buildings. It awarded an additional prize of $200 to the league with the most beautiful grounds and buildings.

Meanwhile, residents of the 1,300-family Calder Community League were outraged over their treatment by city administration. J. C. Beckett, the league's president, complained about inadequate police protection in the area, particularly given his opinion that the district seemed to have been taken over by a group of teenage hooligans. He also reprimanded the administration for poor street lighting, neglected streets, delays in getting telephone service to residents, and continuing complications in the payment of utility fees. (Calder residents had to go downtown, 8 kilometres (5 miles) away, to pay their civic bills, while residents of other communities could pay them at a financial institution within their area.)

A well-organized petition highlighted the concerns of Calder residents and pressed the matter at city hall, where it quickly received attention and Mayor Harry Ainlay's sympathetic ear. Within weeks, he acknowledged that the league residents had valid concerns, which he promised to rectify as soon as possible. Council immediately approved the institution of a "resident policeman" in the area, the establishment of street lights along 127th Avenue (between 118th and 123rd-A streets), the re-establishment of street-library service, and a mechanism for Calder residents to pay their city bills at the local Treasury Branch. The city also promised the extension of telephone services and the improvement of roadways, but not in the immediate future. However, the city declined the league's request for more wooden sidewalks, because it had run out of nails.

Meanwhile, the Edmonton Recreation Commission scored a first, by opening playschool programs in several parts of the city. Using community halls and churches, the programs offered a variety of play activities to preschool-aged children. One step short of the kindergarten model, the playschool program first appeared in September 1946 at the Westmount Community Hall. (Marion Spencer established Alberta's first kindergarten program in 1969 at the McLeod Community League.) Thanks to the recreation commission, the program expanded in 1947 to the Forest Heights, Jasper Place, and Riverdale districts. The Jasper Place Community League also undertook to sponsor a three-day carnival during the May long weekend. The event, located at the recreation grounds, featured a variety of activities including wrestling, boxing, dancing, races, games, and an open-air concert.

By late May, the EFCL and its leagues received a much-needed financial boost from the city, which approved a special grant to assist the leagues in building their halls or other structures. Authored by Alderman Athlestan Bisset, the grant offered leagues a maximum of $5,000 or 20 percent of the total cost of the structure—provided the leagues were not adequately served by other structures (such as a school), would build the new structure on land leased from the city, and would allow "reasonable use" of the building for programs operated by the recreation commission.

By the summer of 1948, the city was abuzz with the construction of playgrounds. Funded through community leagues as well as the Gyro Club, these playgrounds offered an increasing range of activities to a growing number of youngsters. This was highly encouraged by many, but by none more than Constable D. R. "Doc" McNaughton, the city's probation officer. He complained that the youth of the day were not receiving attention or direction from their parents. He commended the efforts of the EFCL and the leagues, but also noted that a certain segment of the population did not take part in league activities. Some young boys within that segment of the population seemed idle, without sufficient supervision, and risked getting into mischief. Vandalism was a major and growing problem for the leagues. Determined to correct the situation, McNaughton joined the EFCL to achieve his goal.

Convinced that the solution for the problem was the creation of a summer camp for disadvantaged children from Edmonton and area, he then assumed the task of organizing youth activities for the summer months. Despite many a naysayer, McNaughton found a site for the camp near the junction of the Sturgeon and North Saskatchewan rivers. Owned by Ed Fordham, a Fort Saskatchewan farmer, the 3-hectare (7-acre) parcel of land was rough, rocky, densely covered with bush, and of little value for farming. However, as it was visited by a variety of wildlife, covered with berry bushes, and located near a river where fishing was good, the land was perfect for a summer camp. It also had tremendous historical significance. According to Bowler and Wanchuk, the site was near the spot "where Anthony Henday, the first white man to visit Alberta, made a stopover on his journey from the Rocky Mountains to the Hudson's Bay in 1754" (p. 89).

McNaughton's conviction about the value of the camp and his determination were infectious. Soon many volunteers and donors came forth to assist in making the dream a reality. Ed Fordham, who had little use for that segment of his farm, offered the EFCL its use as a camp on the condition that the EFCL would pay the taxes on the land. The EFCL readily accepted Fordham's offer as well as support from the Cosmopolitan Club, which came forward with much-needed funds and support. When work began on the camp in the summer of 1948, a local company, Okos Construction, donated the use of a driver and a bulldozer to extend the local road into the camp area and clear the land along the river to establish a beach area. The Canadian army soon got into the act too, directing Edmonton civilians, who attended driver-training courses and used army trucks to haul sand for a proper beach area.

McNaughton was infatigable in his determination to promote the camp. That summer he talked to anyone who would listen about the camp, its construction, and its needs. Soon there were more donors. According to Bowler and Wanchuk, "the Garneau Community League donated a cabin; the RCAF donated three cabins; other cabins came from the Active Club, and the Sherbrooke, Westmount, and Eastwood community leagues. The army donated several tents" (p. 90). The camp soon boasted its own nurse as well as a cook (who had previously cooked for the U.S. Army). Additionally, a member of the recreation commission, John (Jack) Reilly, volunteered his time to conduct the sports activities at the camp.

The camp's first summer was a study in improvisation. The boys tented along the river and spent much time on "camp improvements." Their positive experiences fuelled publicity that McNaughton and another key camp supporter, Fred Weber, generated. EFCL president Charles Simmonds, fondly referred to as "Mr. Boysdale," soon became a major supporter of the camp. He took over the lead role and became the camp's guiding force, insisting that the camp remain true to its original purpose and meet the needs of disadvantaged kids.

In its first ten years of operation, more than 2,000 boys attended the Boysdale Camp, some for more than one summer. Their stay at the camp was made more successful through the Boys and Girls Club of Edmonton, which provided the programming for the camp. (The Boys and Girls Club continued its support and involvement at the camp for nearly forty years.)

By 1958, the EFCL had decided to expand the camp significantly. It spent $12,500 to purchase approximately an additional 70 hectares (173 acres) from Ed Fordham and his son. A year later, the EFCL recouped the full amount when it sold nearly 23 hectares (56 acres) of the land. Meanwhile, the camp continued to attract more and more attention and support. In 1959, members of the RCMP "K" Division and players of the Edmonton Flyers hockey team visited Boysdale. In the years that followed, the camp continued to grow and serve as a proud reflection of the community league movement. Admittedly, the camp's evolution and the relationship between its organizers and the EFCL were not always smooth. Nevertheless, the camp has remained open every summer except in 2003, when it ran into operational difficulties.

The EFCL and its leagues had achieved much during this era. The creation of the Boysdale Camp aside, three other project accomplishments are worthy of note: the soapbox derby, the carnival queen contest, and the talent show. The first EFCL derby occurred during the Labour Day weekend of September 1946 and was an instant success for participants and spectators alike. Held at McDougall Hill, the event was part of a variety show that included musical rides, dancers, and a display of model aircraft. Within a few years, attendance grew to over 10,000 and the number of participants increased steadily. It was an important civic event, and the mayor routinely presided over its opening ceremonies. Three years later it became a provincial event. However, the involvement of contestants from other parts of the province seemed to remove the close-community nature of past derbies. Attendance wavered and became irregular, dropping to around 4,500 for a few years before rebounding in 1954, when the race, held for the first time on Connor's Hill, broke an all-time record with an estimated 15,000 spectators. (In September 2004, as part of Edmonton's centenary celebration, the EFCL re-enacted the soapbox derby.)

The EFCL carnival queen contests held a similar attraction for Edmonton residents. The tradition of a community league-selected "queen" began in 1917 at the 142nd Street and district community league. (The first carnival queen was Marion Sanders.) The annual event, traditionally held during May Day festivities, grew and evolved over the years. In 1932, the federation began sponsoring a winter carnival and included the selection of its queen as part of that event. On March 28, 1950, mayor and council declared the EFCL-elected carnival queen no longer "Miss Edmonton." In 1952, the EFCL opened the competition to citywide entries, no longer limited to the community leagues. According to EFCL President Charles Simmonds, quoted in the *Edmonton Journal* on March 14, 1952, the new arrangement was "to prove 'that Edmonton can produce the best-looking girls in Canada'." (In 1965, the Miss Edmonton contest became part of the EFCL ice show. It continued under this arrangement until 1981.)

The EFCL winter carnivals, often held in February, were also popular with Edmonton's residents. In its early years, the event involved speed skaters and typically presented an opportunity to showcase graduates of the EFCL-run figure skating program. However, the winter carnival soon grew and received recognition from a wide array of sources. In 1933, for example, the event

The Riverdale Community
League May Queen, 1947.
City of Edmonton Archives
EA 600-75.

An Oliver Community League skating party, 1948.
City of Edmonton Archives EA 600-861C.

included an appearance by Marion McCarthy, who was a member of Canada's 1932 Winter Olympics team at Lake Placid, New York. A year later, the Alberta provincial champions in ski jumping and cross-country skiing made an appearance. In 1938, the indoor skating champions of the Alberta Skating Association were at the event. In 1941, the event's growing success and increasing attendance resulted in its becoming a two-day event. By 1949, it featured a unique parade on city-flooded streets at 101st Street and McDougall Drive. The *pièce de résistance* for the EFCL organizers occurred in 1951, when the event involved a guest appearance by Barbara Ann Scott, Canada's reigning figure skating queen. Scott was a winner of the world, Olympic, European, North American, and Canadian figure skating championships. She delighted the organizers and city residents by being involved in numerous activities during her four days in Edmonton. Later, in the 1960s, the show evolved to adopt a different theme each year.

In 1952, the EFCL decided to display the musical and artistic talent of its community league residents. It created the EFCL Talent Show, which became a massive project for its volunteers. Its key advocate was Ben Hager, who was on the EFCL board of directors as chair of its education committee.

The concept for the talent show originated in 1950, in the Calder Community League, through the effort of a Boy Scout leader called Ernest Cooper. He organized the neighbourhood-focused event, which Hager attended almost by accident. Hager was quickly inspired to champion the expansion of the show to citywide level under the auspices of the EFCL. He enlarged the education committee, which he chaired, to also include Mary Collins, Isabel Hughson, Harold Percival (H. P.) Brown (another EFCL past president), and Ernest Cooper. Together they set out to establish the EFCL Talent Show, which in 2005 continues to be an annual event displaying Edmonton's artistic talent.

Ben Hager was born in 1892 in Salem, Oregon. In 1898, his father, a Baptist minister, moved the family to Edmonton. Hager lived in Edmonton until 1920, when he left to teach in Josephburg, a short distance northeast of the city. He returned a year later to settle in Edmonton's Riverdale District. Hager served various roles on the EFCL board, including as its president from 1932 to 1934.

Marek Jablonski was born in Poland in 1939. By age four he had begun picking out tunes on the piano, and at age six he started formal training at the Krakow Conservatory. Having lost all of their possessions during the war, the Jablonski family moved to Edmonton in 1949, where young Marek played on a neighbour's piano.

In 1951, he received his first scholarship from the Women's Music Club, and a year later, he received a piano from the Active Club. He continued to win music festivals and auditions, and in 1957, he won a scholarship to a summer school in Aspen, Colorado. There he met Rosina Lhevinne and was invited to become her pupil at the Juilliard School of Music in New York. By age twenty-one, he had begun a routine of concert tours, which included Canada, the United States, the U.S.S.R., and South America. Jablonski married an Edmontonian and returned often to the city where his fame had started.

The first EFCL-sponsored talent show took place in 1951 and proved promising. Sixty contestants entered, each one a winner of his or her own league-sponsored show. Contestants competed in a variety of categories including vocal, instrumental, dance, acrobatic activities, and elocution. The event grew year after year and provided an incredible opportunity to many budding performers. The first among many talented winners was Marek Jablonski, who represented the Crestwood Community League and later became one of Canada's renowned pianists.

The talent show provided enormous benefits. It created an alternative program for the sports and recreational activities hosted by the federation or its leagues. It promoted the arts, encouraged youth participation, provided performers with exposure that led to subsequent opportunities, and supplied broad-based entertainment. As always with EFCL- or league-sponsored activities, these shows materialized through the effort of volunteers.

Around 1957, an idea took shape that resulted in the Spring Variety Show. Possibly inspired by the talent show, the Elmwood Park Community League

Helen Richards was very active in the Elmwood Community League Spring Variety Show and served it through many roles. She moved to the area with her air force veteran husband and bought a house in Greirson Estates, a neighbourhood that became home to the Elmwood Park Community League. She recalls that each veteran received one-third of an acre (about one-tenth of a hectare) of land, there were four houses to a block, and the cost of league membership in the mid-1950s was a dollar.

(Grierson Estates) initiated the Spring Variety Show to raise funds for its programs. The league recruited Jack Unwin, Edmonton's "Mr. Show Business," as director. Countless league volunteers filled a wide range of roles, including acting as singers, dancers, actors, set designers, costume makers, and beer waiters, to make the show possible. The show started as a weekend production. The show lasted for more than twenty years, and grew into ten performances spread over five weekends. These events were popular and typically sold out three months ahead of performance date.

During this era, the EFCL continued to be active on many other fronts. In the early 1950s, with the dawning of the nuclear age and East–West tension, the Department of National Defence recruited the EFCL to assist with the department's civil defence responsibilities. After hearing a presentation in January 1951 by Brigadier General J. C. Jefferson about the situation and its demands, the EFCL began to organize its leagues into what the Edmonton Journal referred to as "self-contained defense units" (January 23, 1951). Jefferson assisted the EFCL in developing an educational program for league volunteers regarding first aid and protection from possible nuclear attacks or radiation. Air-raid wardens, similar to those established during the last war, again appeared across the city. A year later, more than a thousand individuals had registered in the program, which appeared to grow. However, with time and a decline in the sense of urgency, the program, and participation in it, slowly faded away.

For the EFCL, there were other battles to be fought. As early as April 1949, the EFCL petitioned the city to grant community leagues a ninety-nine-year lease for the land they occupied and used for playgrounds, community halls, and ice rinks. At that time, the leagues had only a ten-year lease, which was up for renewal. Understandably, the situation left the leagues concerned or anxious about their investment in the local infrastructure, as well as about their continued ability to conduct their increasingly popular programs. The debate became intense and emotional. The EFCL argued that the leagues needed a more certain future, without the risk that the infrastructure they had built so carefully through their volunteers be overtaken by the city. City administration, on the other hand, argued that a century would bring so much change that the city needed to avoid creating a policy it could not easily change or sustain.

At the heart of the lease-renewal battle was the city's proposed reduction to the land holdings of each league. The intent of the city's strategy was to limit the league-operated land to the footprint actually occupied by the league's building. Naturally, the EFCL took the stand that the lease renewal should occur without any land-size reduction. Discussion on this matter continued during much of 1951 without resolution. Some league presidents became extremely frustrated with the situation and were prepared to turn over their community hall keys to the city. They could not understand why the city would ignore their voluntary contributions. (The July 13 issue of the *Edmonton Journal* noted: "It had been computed that it would cost $300,000 a year to provide the services to children which the leagues now offer.")

Then, on October 5, the *Journal* reported that the city's legal department was drafting a new lease agreement. According to the article, Mayor Sid Parsons stated that each league would have its own lease agreement and that the leases would soon be forwarded to the EFCL to coordinate their signing by the thirty-four leagues.

A somewhat related issue was the fact that community league constitutions did not specify each league's geographical boundaries. D. R. McNaughton, the EFCL youth and welfare director, raised the matter at the EFCL's November general meeting. He recommended the creation of a special committee to study the current boundaries and recommend a new set of guidelines for the establishment of league boundaries. The problem appeared to exist in older or established leagues as well as in new ones. In some cases, the leagues simply expanded into each other's territory with obvious overlap. Others were growing unopposed, but without guidance as to their future size limits. (In time, this initiative established an orderly set of boundaries that continues to exist today.)

A further complication to this matter was the involvement of the Edmonton Recreation Commission, which was trying to assert itself and evolve from its initial advisory role to become a civic department. The recreation commission argued in favour of a "go slow" approach and the study of the matter before making a decision. By November 1949, the EFCL and the recreation commission were trying to patch up their differences and establish a strategy for the coordination of all phases of recreation and athletic activities.

At the same time, however, EFCL president Charles Simmonds complained about a proposed bylaw that would create a new recreation commission with almost complete powers over all aspects of recreation. According to the November 12 issue of the Edmonton Journal, many EFCL members were concerned that the proposed new bylaw would "kill all volunteer effort and destroy the individual and fine community spirit of every league." Simmonds stated, "Since the recreation commission was first organized we have cooperated in a splendid development of recreation programs." The key message was to leave the recreation commission alone. Eventually, city officials heard the message.

In April 1950, the EFCL and its youth director, D. R. McNaughton, scored another coup. The Edmonton Journal (April 15, 1950) quoted him asking, "What does the youth of Edmonton want most of all?" The answer was the creation of a new EFCL citywide program that provided crafts and trades training for city youth. The idea quickly got the attention of the private sector, which donated shop time and space as well as instructors. The program became an instant success. One woodworking-skill instructor, Edward Webb, offered his shop free of charge one night a week. He prepared for a maximum of 24 participants, but on the first night, 175 boys appeared, ready and eager to take his course.

These courses were attractive because they were given free of charge to the boys, with all materials being paid for by the EFCL. However, their other attraction was the variety of topics offered. In addition to woodworking, the federation provided courses on automotives, electricity, photography, welding, and even radio training, which McNaughton had organized through the military. McNaughton was convinced that this program would curtail juvenile delinquency. He put much of his attention and energy to expanding the program, which became so successful that it even attracted men who were looking for trade training.

Other issues prevailed through the period ending in 1960. These resulted in the federation taking a stand in favour of greater use of school facilities, reduced taxation on the leagues, reduced class sizes in the public schools, reduced vandalism, and increased safety. The latter involved the EFCL, starting in 1954, in the delivery of "pedal-pusher" bicycle-safety training to young children. The program was extremely popular, and by 1955 more than 1,000 children aged eight to twelve had learned about bicycle safety rules and maintenance from community volunteers. Steve Chahley of the Edmonton Safety Council, who was also chairman of the federation's safety committee, first trained these volunteers.

In July 1957, the EFCL received a citation from the U.S. National Recreation Association (headquartered in New York) for the federation's outstanding service to the recreation program in Edmonton. The Edmonton Recreation Board, an affiliated member of the National Recreation Association, nominated the federation. The citation was the culmination of nearly forty years of dedicated effort by countless volunteers to significantly enhance the quality of life in Edmonton. It recognized the federation's potential and was a great motivator for the growing organization.

By November 1958, the federation included sixty-three leagues plus five affiliates in the Jasper Place area. In addition, the federation assisted a number of rural leagues and Calgary area leagues through their formation. This effort toward Calgary's budding league organization was significant and established a close relationship, which is still strong today. During that year, the EFCL membership elected Charles Simmonds for his eleventh consecutive term as president! In 1958, he led a reorganization of the EFCL into five zones along the lines of the city-established parks and recreation boundaries. One president from the leagues in each zone was elected vice-president, and brought the zone's issues to the EFCL executive.

A year later, in December 1959, the federation undertook another first when it published the first issue of its magazine, *Community Life*, which became a quarterly publication. The first issue had eighty pages and sold for fifty cents. It covered all aspects of community league operations, with emphasis on recreation and sports. Charles Simmonds, EFCL president and the magazine's editor, was quoted in the *Edmonton Journal* (January 6, 1960) as saying that the magazine was based to some degree on the recreation magazine of the National Recreation Association. The magazine contained words of welcome and

congratulation from Mayor (and Dr.) Elmer E. Roper and Premier Ernest Manning. The premier wrote, "It is a sign of maturity when the members of an organized group seek to enshrine the story of their activities, in print, through the medium of their own publication."

During 1959, the EFCL was part of another significant event in the city's history—the Joint Use Agreement, a formal agreement between the City of Edmonton, Edmonton Public Schools, and Edmonton Catholic Schools. The Joint Use Agreement, finalized in 1959 and revised most recently in 1996, made school facilities available to community groups during after-school hours. In exchange, city facilities such as arenas, pools, museums, and the like became available to schoolchildren during school hours. The agreement clarified how the three partners were to work together to design, build, and maintain school and park sites.

The mechanics of this agreement evolved from the late 1940s, when the recreation commission had received permission to schedule the use of school grounds (on a permit basis) after 6:00 p.m. during school days and on weekends. The commission also received access to indoor school facilities for a nominal fee. The first cooperative school–park development took place at Ross Sheppard High School and Coronation Park in the 1950s, leading to the first joint agreement to share the costs of developing and maintaining school grounds.

Initially signed by the City of Edmonton and the Edmonton Public School Board, in 1966 the Tri-Partite Agreement extended to include Edmonton's Separate (i.e., Catholic) School Board. In the ensuing decades, the agreement evolved and progressed. It included the establishment of guidelines or agreements related to joint development of sites, the continued operation and maintenance of school parks, the undertaking of cost analyses, and the development of guidelines for facility use.

An extensive review of the Tri-Partite Agreement conducted in 1995 resulted in the current agreement, signed in 1996. It noted, "The City and the Boards acknowledge that it is the shared goal of the parties to ensure that the School Sites and the Parks and Recreation Sites are made available for the use and enjoyment of the citizens of the City of Edmonton and that the School Sites and the Park and Recreation Sites are accessible to the public." Additionally, it incorporated a committee structure to ensure the involvement of community users and stakeholders, and established a set of agreed principles to guide its effort. These principles included shared use, cooperative planning, consultation, efficiency and effectiveness, and shared cost.

By the end of the 1950s, the EFCL was well on its way to formalizing a number of sports programs across the city. Its various committees and countless volunteers addressed the spectrum of activities from recreation to competitive sports. The federation established a sports-related structure that included playing zones, leagues and tournaments. While figure skating and hockey often dominated the EFCL's attention, the federation also dabbled in wrestling, boxing, and speed skating. By the late 1940s, soccer was also a major activity. These activities created a strong foundation for the federation as it and Edmonton progressed into their next stage of growth.

If there is no dull and determined effort,
there will be no brilliant achievement.

– HSUN-TZU

5

Growth, Immigration, and Prosperity

1961–1987

Doing nothing for others is the undoing of ourselves.
— HORACE MANN

T HE POST-WAR PERIOD LEADING TO THE 1960s was a period of growth that appeared to go on forever. At least, that was the perception at the time. During that era, Edmonton grew in all aspects and times were good. Office towers, hotels, and skyscrapers materialized out of nowhere to command attention across the downtown skyline. In the suburbs, shopping centres, hotels, motels, fancy residences, and entertainment facilities sprouted to fill the landscape and fuel the city's expansion. The value of building permits in 1958 totalled $72.5 million; by 1970, that figure had nearly doubled to $136.7 million. Person (1981) reported, "By 1971 the city was attracting one new manufacturing plant every five and a half days" (p. 206).

From 1956 to 1971, the city's population grew from 226,000 to more than 436,000. This growth had some external triggers like increased immigration to Canada and growing urbanization; however, a major force in the population growth was the strong and vibrant economy across Alberta and in Edmonton. The twin engines of oil and natural gas served to fuel a strong economy that kept expanding through the period. The discovery of additional producing fields in northern Alberta nearly doubled the number of these wells and created an insatiable demand for a variety of jobs.

Edmonton street scene
along 100 Street, 1965.
City of Edmonton Archives
EA 275-118.

The flurry of oil- or gas-related activity in the Edmonton area during the late 1940s and 1950s received a boost from the construction, in Fort McMurray, of the first commercial oil sands plant in the world. Located to the southwest, Edmonton served as Fort McMurray's only viable gateway and service centre. When production of synthetic crude oil started in 1967, Edmonton continued to benefit through the additional construction of a network of pipelines and the expansion of refineries. Edmonton also benefited from the development of lead and zinc mines in Pine Point, and the expansion of the Northern Alberta Railways to carry the ore to faraway markets.

In short, employment was readily available and brought about a sense of expansiveness born by readily available disposable funds. Public and private money flowed more readily than at any other time in Edmonton's history, encouraged by the continued expansion of the current technology and its array of gadgets, and the increasing choices for consumers.[1]

The prosperity of the 1950s brought about cars that were longer, lower to the ground, sleeker-looking (with fins and chrome), and faster than ever before. Edmonton's residents were attracted to these cars, and soon their city had the highest ratio of cars per capita on the continent. (The last serving horse-drawn milk wagon in Edmonton retired on May 11, 1961. The delivery vans that replaced the wagons lasted for a while, but milk delivery in Edmonton went by the boards soon after.) The growth in car usage brought about many concerns for traffic safety as well as for the flow of traffic across the North Saskatchewan River. The city built four new bridges—Quesnell (1968), Capilano (1969), James MacDonald (1971), and Beverly (twinned in 1972). Many of the older bridges underwent upgrades.

The demand for travel between the two cities increased steadily and placed much pressure on Edmonton's one and only airport at Blatchford Field. As the demand for air travel increased, especially with Edmonton's northern links, it soon became necessary to establish a bigger airport, and the Edmonton International Airport was built near Leduc, some distance south of Edmonton. Blatchford Field was renamed the Industrial Airport and became the focus of national and private flights. Edmonton also saw the birth of Wardair, the airline created by the famous bush pilot Max Ward, who in 1961 acquired an international charter licence to fly Canadians around the world.

On May 22, 1963, Pacific Western Airlines, Canada's third largest airline, inaugurated an airbus service between Calgary and Edmonton. The three flights per day cost $11 each way. By 1981, passengers could select from nineteen daily flights, which cost $50.95 each way. A few years earlier, on April 22, 1978, Edmonton proudly opened its Light Rail Transit (LRT) system, connecting northeast neighbourhoods to the downtown core. (The term light refers to the reduced rail-car weight, the speed, and the load capacity of the system.) Completed in four years, the $65-million project was North America's first LRT system and Canada's third rapid transit system. One of the greatest achievements in the development of the LRT was its construction underneath Jasper Avenue. The project attracted much attention because it involved a novel engineering technique that allowed for minimal disruption of traffic across this main street and to the businesses along its path. In 1981, the LRT extended to the Clareview area, and in 1984, it connected to the Legislature Building. Planning included additional rail branches; however, because of their high cost, the city deferred their construction.

The 1960s saw a tremendous growth in the demand for education and training. This thirst for knowledge stemmed in part from the rapid evolution of technology and the processes used in production, transportation, finance, or management. Everything seemed to be becoming more structured or systemic. Other triggers involved increases in disposable income, enhanced competition for "good" jobs, and a continued faith in a better future.

These triggers brought about an explosion in the education sector. The baby-boom generation filled the school system to the brim, and use of portable classrooms became a common practice to augment the capacity of older schools. The number of adult students also increased and nearly doubled the University of Alberta's enrolment, forcing it to expand its facilities. But that was not enough to meet the demand, and soon a new player, the Northern Alberta Institute of Technology (NAIT), joined the local scene. Shortly after it opened on a 11-hectare (26-acre) site just east of the Industrial Airport, NAIT became, in size and student population, the largest polytechnic institute in Canada.

A craving for the arts and professional sports complemented the thirst for education. Slowly but surely, professional artistic endeavours established and complemented the Women's Musical Club Celebrity Concerts, the EFCL Talent Show, and other musical ventures that had been around for a while. The Edmonton Symphony Orchestra, inactive through most of the war, reappeared in 1952 to become fully professional and gain Canada-wide recognition. In 1959, the Ukrainian Shumka Dancers formed and within fifteen years gained international renown. The Alberta Ballet Company formed in 1962, and a year later the Edmonton Professional Opera formed, entertaining Edmonton and area residents with high-quality performances.

Other artistic ventures flourished and increased the range of artistic expression that the locals could experience.[2] The Citadel Theatre, Edmonton's first professional theatre, opened in 1965 and quickly gained national acclaim for the quality of its productions. Others followed suit. Amateur theatre groups, which had long been a part of Edmonton, began to expand. They included the Studio Theatre, Torches Theatre, and the Walterdale Playhouse. The new art gallery, donated by Dr. and Mrs. W. N. Condell, opened in 1969 and was followed shortly afterward by a host of private art galleries.

Edmonton's first television broadcast occurred on Sunday, October 17, 1954, through the Sunwapta Broadcasting Company located in the West End. In the ensuing three years, Sunwapta Broadcasting (and its CFRN-TV counterpart) was linked to a microwave network, and on October 5, 1957, it offered its

The Ukrainian Shumka Dancers troupe started in 1959 with only sixteen dancers. Its first director, Chester Kuc, helped shape the organization for its first ten years. (He then moved on to organize the Ukrainian Cheremosh Dance Ensemble and the Ukrainian National Federation School of Dancing.) By 1981, the troupe had sixty dancers and a twenty-four-piece orchestra whose conductor-arranger served in 2004 as Alberta's minister of community development and deputy house leader—Gene Zwozdesky.

The troupe had a long string of successes, performing at the Montreal Expo in 1967, representing Canada at various international festivals, and playing at the opening ceremonies of the 1978 Commonwealth Games in Edmonton. Another success during that year was the invitation the troupe received to dance a command performance for Her Majesty Queen Elizabeth II.

viewers their first live broadcast—the World Series. A second TV channel, CBXT, began broadcasting in 1961 as the new CBC affiliate. Colour broadcasting began in Edmonton on October 1, 1966. A third station, Channel 11, the CBC French-language station, began its broadcasts on March 1, 1970. Because it shared its network with the English-language programming of the Metropolitan Edmonton Educational Television Association (MEETA), Channel 11 became Canada's first bilingual channel. By 1976, Edmonton's residents could choose from twelve different television stations.

The Edmonton Exhibition Grounds were also wildly popular for their entertainment. In 1962, a new theme, the 1898 Klondike Gold Rush, appeared at the grounds. This caught the imagination of Edmonton's residents and visitors alike and made the "Klondike Days" celebration one of the ten most popular festivals in North America. The event, which still occurs annually, provides a variety of activities for all ages including relatively recent additions such as the sourdough raft race and the promenade. Collectively, these have sparked the interest of the community at large and spawned a variety of activities that annually transform the city into its glory days of the Klondike.

Another entertainment centre, the Edmonton International Speedway, opened
in May 1967. The 120-hectare (300-acre) facility west of 127th Street and 137th
Avenue was one of the most comprehensive auto-racing facilities in Canada. Car
racing was not new to Edmonton. Such races, held at the Exhibition Grounds during
the 1920s, died out during the Depression and World War II. The races revived in
1949 and rapidly grew in popularity. The facility hosted Can-Am Group 7 car races
as well as drag races of world-championship calibre. With time, the popularity of the
facility waned, and the last major race occurred in 1973. However, in 1981, Peter
Pocklington, a wealthy local sportsman, revived the Can-Am races at the speedway.

Growing prosperity, wealth, and optimism also had a significant bearing
on local consumers. This attracted the attention of the business sector, which
increased in numbers and shopping opportunities. New shopping malls
appeared, the most notable of the era being Southgate Shopping Mall. When it
opened on August 11, 1970, at 111th Street and 51st Avenue, the $25-million
facility was the largest shopping centre west of Toronto. It was the first time that
two of Canada's largest retail companies, the Hudson's Bay Company and
Woodward's, teamed up in the same mall complex.

Premier Peter Lougheed and Mayor Laurence Decore with the Stanley Cup, 1988.
City of Edmonton Archives EA 340-1387.

Wealth was indeed growing rapidly. In the summer of 1971, a Conservative government headed by Peter Lougheed ousted the Social Credit government of Harry E. Strom, who had assumed the premiership from the elder Ernest Manning. Premier Lougheed was a lawyer and the grandson of Calgary-based senator James Lougheed. A shrewd and popular politician, the younger Lougheed quickly raised the royalties charged to oil companies, so that within two years the government's net revenue from oil and gas doubled to an annual rate of $500 million. At the same time, the increasing provincial oil reserves gave Alberta and its capital city a rosy future. Alberta was processing more than 85 percent of Canada's fossil fuel, making it the centre of the Canadian energy sector. Two years later, in late 1973, amidst a period of perceived oil shortages, Alberta's worth significantly increased again through rising world oil prices.

Growth occurred in other sectors as well. The growing demand for paper products accelerated the growth of the forest industry. Moreover, increasing demands for electrical power triggered the construction (through most of the 1980s) of the 800-megawatt Genesee Power Plant, west of Edmonton. It complemented other coal-powered plants that were located within a 40-kilometre (25-mile) radius from Edmonton. The plants tapped into the world's second largest coal reserve, located in the western Alberta foothills, and revived the mining sector that was in decline following World War II. Edmonton's geographical location established it as the centre for these industries, and it soon reaped the benefits of increased employment and business.

As expected, Alberta and Edmonton became attractive destinations for business and those seeking employment. From 1971 to 1980, the city's population increased from 496,000 to 665,000 people, with expectations that it would double by 2000. That led to a corresponding increase of the city's area from 310 square kilometres (120 square miles) to more than double through the annexation of an additional 347 square kilometres (134 square miles), making Edmonton the city with the largest area in Canada.

Predictably, Edmonton enjoyed a great deal of construction during the era and especially during the 1970s. Twenty-six new office buildings appeared in Edmonton's downtown during that decade, including the AGT Tower, the Imperial Oil building, Edmonton House, the Petroleum Plaza towers, and the four towers of Edmonton Centre. New buildings also appeared at the University of Alberta, where in 1976 enrolment topped 20,000 full-time students. The Northlands Coliseum, the Muttart Conservatory, the Edmonton Convention Centre, the Law Courts building, and a new facility for the Citadel Theatre augmented Edmonton's treasured facilities. Countless residential towers arose in the downtown core. Numerous strip malls, seniors complexes, apartment buildings, and the largest mall in the world—West Edmonton Mall—were constructed. During the 1980s, many historical sites in the downtown were demolished to allow for construction, most notably the Scotia Place complex. These and many other construction projects steadily increased the total value of building permits, which in 1978 rose to over $1 billion.

Edmonton had many proud "firsts" during this era. It was the first city to establish a fibre optic telephone system, the only city in North America (at the time) to establish its own research park for resource development, and the city with the largest central park in North America.

The idea for the development of Edmonton's river valley came from Fredrick G. Todd, a landscape architect from Montreal, in 1907. He suggested that the city council of the time set aside the river valley for a long string of

Edmonton skyline viewed from south of downtown, 1982.
City of Edmonton Archives EA 160-1675.

parks. Though accepted in 1915, the idea became a reality only in 1974, through a joint venture by the three levels of government—municipal, provincial, and federal. Each contributed $12 million to create a natural park, 16 kilometres (10 miles) long, on both sides of the river. The 1,200-hectare (3,000-acre) park included 29 kilometres (18 miles) of paved bicycle trails, 26 kilometres (16 miles) of gravelled hiking trails, and four footbridges across the river, as well as countless benches, fountains, shelters, picnic sites, bicycle racks, and educational signs. The park, which became known as the Ribbon of Green, opened officially on July 8, 1978, and has since continued to be developed.

Then there was the glory of the Commonwealth Games, which Edmonton hosted in 1978. The first Commonwealth Games took place in 1930 in Hamilton, Ontario. In 1954, when it again became Canada's turn to host the games, Vancouver was the chosen venue. On August 3, 1978, it was Edmonton's turn to assume the world stage for an impressive showing of the city's capacity. In attendance were Her Majesty the Queen, numerous other dignitaries, and countless Canadians. The games involved 1,900 athletes from forty-six countries, and an estimated 500 million viewers watched the events on television.

It was a shining moment for Edmonton, which relied on over 10,000 volunteers to make the games a success. The games' lasting legacy for Edmonton includes the 42,900-seat Commonwealth Stadium, an aquatic centre, a firing range in south Edmonton, a velodrome, bowling greens, and some residential space at the University of Alberta, which hosted the athletes. A few years later the university was again in the spotlight when it hosted the World University Games in July 1983.

This era closed with an unfortunate event that left a lasting impact on the city and its residents. The best account comes from an Alberta Public Safety Services 1991 publication entitled *Tornado: A Report.*

> On the afternoon of Friday, July 31, 1987, a tornado ripped through the eastern part of Edmonton and parts of neighbouring Strathcona County. The tornado remained on the ground for an hour, cutting a path of destruction 40 kilometres (25 miles) long and up to a kilometre (0.6 miles) wide in places, and reaching wind speeds up to 420 km (260 miles) per hour. The tornado killed 27 people, injured hundreds, destroyed more than 300 homes, and caused more than $330 million in property damage at four major disaster sites. The loss of life, injuries and destruction of property made it the worst natural disaster in Alberta's recent history, and one of the worst in Canada's history. (p. i)

The period between 1961 and 1987 was an exciting era of growth and challenges for Alberta, and its capital Edmonton.[3]

༺༄ ༄༺

Amid this growth, the Edmonton Federation of Community Leagues (EFCL) steadily continued its grassroots work along its original theme: the enhancement of the quality of life at community level. Its task continued to be challenging, despite the growing wealth, and continued to stretch the organization, and its volunteers, to new limits.

In 1955, a report on recreation facilities and space in Edmonton recommended that the city's recreation department create sixteen community recreation directors. These directors would be responsible for helping their area community leagues with recreational needs and other responsibilities such as governance. According to Bert Pettigrew, the city's superintendent of recreation, the directors' responsibilities were necessarily broad because "the program needs of each league are different, as are [their] methods of operations and facilities." In the Autumn 1961 issue of the EFCL publication *Community Life*, he identified the following general responsibilities:

1. Know Department and Recreation Board policies.
2. Survey the area and know the community.
3. Work in close co-operation with the league executive and committees, to assist these groups carry out their particular responsibilities.
4. Assist these groups in particular in the areas of facilities, equipment, program activities, recruitment of members, recruitment of leaders, duties of committee personnel, conduct of meetings, training courses for volunteers, civic services, grants, referrals, continuity.
5. Strive to stimulate greater voluntary response by interpretation of aims and objectives, assist with public relations and publicity, talent surveys, and assist with planning for evaluation and recognition of volunteer effort.
6. Arrange for skilled leadership to meet the requested program needs of the community, where volunteer resources are inadequate.
7. Assist with securing facilities or additional facilities to meet demonstrated needs. (p. 5)

In the fall of 1959, the city established six such directors on an experimental basis. The move proved to be a success, and in the fall of 1961, the city decided to establish two more directors, filling the posts in 1962. The lofty and worthwhile aims assigned to the positions went a long way to assist in the efforts of countless volunteers at the local level to ameliorate the overall quality of life in the city. In time, however, this effort gradually dissipated until it almost lost its focus. (Currently, community recreation coordinators focus more on facility construction and program facilitation.)

In February 1961, the EFCL again confronted a major challenge to the integrity of recreational facilities in Edmonton. At its basis was a proposal to consolidate all community recreational space, often within or around school facilities and grounds. The idea won the support of the recreation department and both school boards. Initially the EFCL objected to the idea because the arrangement would restrict the access of league members to the recreational facilities or space, or force the hands of leagues regarding recreational activities. The *Edmonton Journal* (June 15, 1961) quoted EFCL President Charles Simmonds's complaint about the risk of reducing the space available for recreation.

"There is nothing more needed in this city than recreation area," he observed. "We made a policy many years ago which stated a 'hands-off' policy regarding the use of parkland by the city. We spent a good deal of money protesting the building of the Glenora Club in the river flats, and also fought the use of the South Side Athletics Grounds as a site for Strathcona Composite High School."

Simmonds's long list of complaints against the arrangement included the absence of the EFCL in the Joint Planning Committee and its negotiation process, and the existing arrangement whereby the EFCL continues to pay rent for the use of school facilities. Another problem included the various restrictions placed on the use of school space—such as limited hours and the inability to use the space for fundraising activities without a corresponding increase in rent. Nevertheless, faced with much external pressure, the EFCL had little choice but to protest the proposal, live with its consequences, and keep going.

A few months later, in September 1961, amid much fanfare the EFCL celebrated its forty-fifth anniversary. A banquet, held at the Jubilee Auditorium, to "honour the volunteers" was attended by Mayor Elmer Roper, various city council members, and Gordon Taylor, the minister of highways. The event included various award presentations including one to the federation, which received a National Recreation Association of America citation and life membership for its recreation-related service to Edmonton's residents. Ben Hager, federation past president and current chair of the education committee, received a life membership in the EFCL. Hager's award recognized his tremendous dedication and enormous contribution to the community league movement during a thirty-eight-year-long commitment.

By that time, there were seventy-nine leagues across Edmonton, and the matter of league membership drives became a concern for both the EFCL and its leagues.[4] The federation decided to test the idea of a coordinated and synchronized membership drive with the leagues. At the EFCL general meeting that

Bicycle parade, 1963.
EFCL collection.

May, the president of Crestwood, L. Duhamel, moved that the league publicity week occur annually during the third week of September and be followed one week later by the leagues' membership drives. The motion carried with the understanding that the federation would coordinate the publicity and resources required for the membership drives. This practice, which is still in operation today, reduced the overall costs of the membership drive for the leagues, increased their visibility, and enhanced their buying power.

Sports and recreation continued to be a main activity of the EFCL. The September 23, 1961, issue of the *Edmonton Journal* reported: "There's nothing small about minor sport in Edmonton. Last year more than 4,500 children and teenagers took part in community league sponsored sports." The largest segment of the federation effort focused on hockey. According to the same article in the *Journal*, "Last winter 139 teams with 2,500 players operated in four city zones. This number is expected to grow to 200 teams and 3,600 players this season [1961–62]." Given the estimated cost of $300 to outfit each team, the federation's overall effort totalled around $50,000. Yet it was not the sum of its effort or expenses on behalf of sports for Edmonton's children. Baseball ranked second in EFCL funding, and involved nearly 1,100 players in 73 teams from four age divisions. The EFCL also operated 49 fastball teams that catered to 735 players, as well as 86 boxing, weightlifting, and wrestling teams. It held its first novice swim meet at the Mill Creek pool and established a new soccer league in Edmonton's northwest area with expansion planned for the following year.

As it turned out, during the 1960s and 1970s the EFCL spent a great deal of energy, organization, and money to organize its growing sports programs. With the demand for sports rising steadily, pressure increased to organize each sport into an association and allow it some autonomy to mature on its own. Many did, including soccer, hockey, amateur boxing and wrestling, speed skating, and figure skating. Over time, each federation-sponsored sport flourished into its own and became an independent association. (Many are still serving the city's residents.)

The EFCL annual general meeting held on November 8, 1961, was "historical" if for no other reason than the resignation of one of its primary movers and shakers—Charles Simmonds, who declined to stand for re-election. For thirteen years, Simmonds had presided over the EFCL, and he was instrumental in promoting and protecting it as well as in initiating many of its programs. Allan Welsh replaced him. Steve Chahley was elected first vice-president, and Ralph Bechloff became second vice-president.

Things were definitely evolving for the EFCL. During 1962, its office relocated to city hall, where the city provided space as well as an administrative assistant; for the first time, the EFCL had full-time staff. Not to be outdone, the provincial government also got into the act of supporting the federation.

Highway Minister Gordon Taylor was the guest speaker in September at an *Edmonton Journal*–sponsored banquet, held at the Jubilee Auditorium to kick off the annual Community Week, with representatives from the seventy-nine existing leagues. Mayor Elmer Roper became an honorary member of the EFCL and officially proclaimed the membership-drive period a "Community Week." Other dignitaries at the event included representatives from the YWCA and the YMCA, Boy Scouts and Girl Guides, the Journal, and Safeway. According to the *Journal* (September 8, 1962), Mayor Roper stated, "I can't express words adequately enough that express my own satisfaction and appreciation for the work done in the city by the Federation of Community Leagues." The event and the membership drive received extensive coverage by the media. Their stories

Born in England in 1893, Charles Simmonds served with distinction in World War I, where he won the Military Cross and the Croix de Guerre. In 1922, he moved to Kelowna, British Columbia, where he operated a fruit orchard and cattle ranch. He was then involved in the oil business (from Vancouver), life insurance (in Saskatoon, and from 1934 in Edmonton), and since 1951 in real estate, managing his own Edmonton-based business.

In 1948, Simmonds became president of the EFCL. He inherited an organization that had lost some of its early momentum. Its seventeen league members were having difficulty making ends meet financially and operationally, and membership was down across the board. Simmonds was a tireless promoter of the EFCL. He took every opportunity to talk to various organizations—from church groups to business associations—about the benefit of having an all-inclusive grassroots organization that would promote the well-being of Edmonton's residents. His presidency lasted for thirteen years, during which time he initiated numerous programs including the Boysdale Camp, for which he chaired the board of trustees.

During his long community-focused career, Simmonds also served as chair of the Edmonton Recreation Commission, board member of the Community Chest, member of the Edmonton and Alberta Safety Council, member of the Athletic Council of the Edmonton Wrestling and Boxing Commission, member of the Edmonton Exhibition Association, and city alderman for a two-year term.

At the end of his term, the EFCL was fifty-five leagues strong and a well-recognized entity in civic and recreational affairs. For his achievements, Simmonds earned countless awards and distinctions. In May 1962, he was also awarded an EFCL lifetime membership. He died six months later on November 12.

included promotion of the EFCL and encouragement to purchase league membership.

Only a few months later, the EFCL was again on the agenda at city hall, in a clash with Alderman and Deputy Mayor Stan Milner and the council finance committee on one side and EFCL President Allan Welsh on the other. Apparently when Welsh was before the committee seeking increased building grants for the leagues, Milner told Welsh that "the only reason his [Milner's] family has a community league membership is because he was not at home when the league membership canvasser called" (Edmonton Journal, November 23, 1962). Welsh was livid and threatened to resign unless he (and thousands of EFCL volunteers) received an apology from Milner. The matter then festered for a few months, souring the relationship between the EFCL and the city. In the end, Milner apologized to both the EFCL and Welsh.

An article in the Edmonton Journal on September 14, 1963, highlighted the EFCL's service record in the city, noting that the EFCL and its eighty-two leagues had in 1962 involved 165,388 youngsters in community sports and programs, and that "many, many hundreds of children and adults made use of community

Oliver Community League Hockey youth team, circa 1962.
EFCL collection.

league facilities in addition to these organized teams. Thus the community league is a valuable asset to each community." The article went on to list the "tremendous" efforts by the leagues, which strove to:

- maintain and operate over 125 ice rinks, which had an estimated annual attendance of over one million children
- organize and operate nearly 250 hockey teams for over 4,000 players, plus helping more than 2,000 children play unorganized inter-league hockey
- organize and operate 150 fastball and baseball teams involving 2,500 children
- organize and operate the federation Talent Show involving more than 500 children
- operate the Boysdale Camp, (which became a member agency of the United Community Fund of Greater Edmonton), where more than 200 children attended the camp
- provide volunteers for 52 playschools, in a joint venture with the city recreation department

- foster the promotion of friendship clubs, Brownies and Guides, Cubs and Scouts, and other organizations that benefit the community

By December 1963, the EFCL was pressing its point home at city council on two issues: leasing of parkland and the need for an ombudsman's office. The federation protested the leasing of parkland to private clubs following the recent leasing of the Connors Hill and part of the Gallagher Park to the Edmonton Ski Club. The EFCL was concerned that public access to the park area was now restricted and costly. Another issue was the federation's plea to city hall to establish a position of "citizen's defender" or ombudsman. Alderman Ed Leger proposed having the matter studied by the city solicitors; however, his suggestion was defeated by Acting Mayor Ethel Wilson, who tipped the scales of a tie vote.

At around the same time, the EFCL took steps to assist a potentially neglected group of people—Edmonton's needy families. It decided that members of families on social assistance would receive free membership to their community leagues. This created a close partnership between the federation and the city welfare department, the precursor to the current Community Services Department. They agreed that the city welfare department would identify the needy families to the respective league president, who would then ensure that each family received its league membership free of charge. The federation implemented the process rapidly, and it is still subtly in practice today.

Another identified neglected group—youth—became the target of concern for the federation in early 1963. EFCL president Allan Welsh expressed concern about Edmonton's 40,000-plus teenagers. The *Edmonton Journal* (January 3, 1964) reported comments by Welsh and by Hal Thomas, president of the Beverly League, who noted: "When I was a kid there was no such thing as a teenager. We weren't separated from the rest of humanity by this name *teenager*." Both Thomas and Welsh complained that teens had little supervision at home, or elsewhere, and needed a place and a program that would give them structure and role models. They suggested that this structure could be provided at their community hall through league programs, and they encouraged the development of such programs. In the meanwhile, the federation continued with its other programs—the spring clean-up campaign, the talent show, and Boysdale—which gained in popularity.

In January 1964, Mayor William Hawrelak announced the creation of a three-member committee to investigate the relationship (and operations) between the Parks and Recreation Department and the federation as a whole, as well as with each of the leagues. The three members included lawyer Percy Marshall, the Alberta manager for Hiram Walker and Sons, Brigadier Robert A. Bradburn, and Dr. M. L. van Vliet, the director of the University of Alberta physical education department. Their task was attacked immediately and vehemently by the EFCL, which felt their mission was one-sided and inappropriate because it also intended to investigate the relationship between the federation and its individual leagues. At one point, John Long, the federation president, announced that the EFCL was contemplating its own investigation into the relationship between city council and its various departments. While the federation soon dropped its "investigation," its angst about the city's review continued. Nevertheless, 1965 found both the city and the EFCL implementing some of the recommendations made by Mayor Hawrelak's committee.

One of the most significant changes related to area recreational councils, or simply "area councils." The committee believed that the EFCL should establish area councils, each involving five or more leagues with a representative on the EFCL board of directors. It felt that this structural change would benefit both the leagues and the EFCL. The leagues would benefit by having an organization that would better assist them in the coordination of matters of local (versus citywide) concern, or in matters bigger than the capacity of any one league. Area councils also hoped to provide each league with a stronger voice than the leagues would otherwise have on their own. The EFCL hoped that the presence of the area councils would provide it with a more efficient mechanism for coordinating and responding to local needs.

EFCL's anxiety over the area councils was reduced by the understanding that they would take direction from the leagues (or the EFCL), and the expectation that because the city had recommended the new structure it would also support it. This expectation proved accurate, for a while. The problem was the ongoing evolution of the area councils and their growing politicization. (In 1999, the EFCL membership felt it necessary to cast off many of the existing area councils as federation representatives.)

The mayor's committee also recommended that the grant system for the community leagues be streamlined. Prior to then, the city had different grants for different purposes, and the leagues would accordingly seek as much as $150 under a building improvement grant, up to $130 in a utility grant, up to $50 for painting expenses, up to $50 for school facility rental, and an average of $100 annually for community hall rentals. The process was deemed cumbersome and full of red tape and paperwork. In August 1965, a new system was instituted with a unified operating grant that depended on the percentage established by the total of a league's membership against its overall population. A league with less than an 11-percent membership would receive up to $100, while a league with a membership of 50 percent or greater would receive up to $500. The new process significantly simplified the required paperwork, and it continues today.

Meanwhile, community life went on. The greatest community-related coverage by the Edmonton Journal during 1965 was of the fourteenth annual talent show, which attracted more than 1,900 people. Other articles addressed the federation's battle to protect land left to the city by Alexander Cameron Rutherford. The EFCL argued that Rutherford's last will and testament clearly designated the 4-hectare (10-acre) lot along the Mill Creek ravine for parkland purposes only, and not for the city-intended Mill Creek freeway. EFCL Vice-President Thomas Jackson moved that that the EFCL take a stand against such encroachment into recreational space. The motion passed but was ignored by the city, which argued that it had the jurisdiction to use any land for such a project (a transportation route) regardless of the original purpose of the land. In the end, the city went ahead with its plan, although the freeway never evolved.

The EFCL's Boysdale program continued to operate and grow. Construction of new facilities at the camp allowed for the inclusion of more campers in the program. However, while program enhancements occurred at the camp, the relationship between the camp management committee and the EFCL board deteriorated. Stephen Wyker, the Boysdale Camp Committee chair, accused the federation and its league of neglecting the camp.

"The community leagues are only interested in the glory, and not the work associated with Boysdale Camp," he said, according to an article in the July 6 Edmonton Journal. EFCL president George Hughes shot back that "nothing is further from the truth ... [and] the only request for assistance was to help finance the swimming pool" at the camp. He added that a month earlier the EFCL board had voted to write off the balance of the pool's costs and that the "lack of response of community leagues to adopt the maintenance and repair of

Residents playing at the Boysdale camp (undated).
City of Edmonton Archives EA 20-5318.

nine camp houses [as implied by Wyker] was an issue that [had] died two years" earlier. Hughes stated that the EFCL was simply trying to ensure the camp committee operated in an efficient "businesslike manner" and that "we can't have a situation where committee chairmen commit themselves to expenditures for which they are not authorized." The matter recurred many times and consumed much of the EFCL's (and leagues') time, effort, and precious resources.

The year ended on a sad note for the EFCL with the death of one of its founders and long-time promoter—Harold Percy "HP" Brown. He was truly a tremendous community supporter and volunteer extraordinaire, who gave much of himself over many decades to enhance the quality of life in his beloved city. He died on November 17, 1965, at the age of eighty.

By September 1966, when the EFCL held its annual membership drive, there were eighty-two active community leagues. They were expanding in membership, programs, and activities. On September 19, 1966, the *Edmonton Journal* gave extensive coverage to the "value" of the community league movement in Edmonton, reporting that "in 1965 the recreation department expended

Harold Percival Brown was born on March 22, 1886, in Guildford, Surrey, England. He started his business career with the English civil service and then moved to Canada. From 1909 to 1917, he served as secretary to Dr. Harry Smith and was also an accountant for Smith Brothers. He joined the University of Alberta Department of Extension and eventually became visual instruction head. In 1927, Brown started CKUA—a radio station that operated under the auspices of the university. He served as CKUA's first program director and chief announcer.

Brown dedicated himself to the betterment of his community. He helped establish Edmonton's first community league, Jasper Place, and served as the EFCL's first secretary and later as its president. For many years he served as chair of the EFCL's education committee. He also served on the Edmonton branch of the Dickens Fellowship and the Cosmopolitan Club. He was an executive member on the board of the provincial branch of the Red Cross (where he launched the Red Cross water safety program), chairman of the provincial swimming and water safety program, director of the Alberta Safety Council, and a member of the Coordinating Council for Crippled Children, the vestry of St. Paul's Anglican Church, and the Diocesan Board of Religious Education of the church. He founded the Edmonton Film Council and was also the secretary of the Edmonton branch of the National Film Society.

Brown received numerous awards for his service, including a National Recreation Association of America award, a Red Cross citation, and lifetime membership in the EFCL.

just over $3,000,000 on the current operating account. The contribution made by the community leagues towards recreation in this city is of such magnitude, that in order to provide the same facilities and services by professionals alone, without the aid of this volunteer agency, would mean a minimum increase of 50 per cent in the current operating budget, or somewhere between two to three mills based upon the present assessment."

The article illustrated the case using an unidentified league of a middle-income community at the start of its sixth year of operation, noting that in 1965 league volunteers had donated over 10,000 hours of service to the city. Using a nominal cost of $1.50 per hour, the *Journal* went on to calculate that, during its five-year existence, the league had provided the city with over $24,000 in capital and more than $20,000 in recreational operations. Therefore, the leagues had saved the city the equivalent of between $1.7 million and $2 million or more annually. "The community league movement ... does indeed play a major role in recreation of this city. Not only does it result in a cost saving to the city, but it also results in 'Dividends in Better Citizenship'—which is the motto of the [EFCL]."

In 1965, one in three Edmonton residents belonged to a league. By 1968 that ratio translated to over 130,000 residents. A brochure produced for the 1965 Community Week inaugural dinner had a short piece by Burton Margolus, the EFCL membership chairman. It reflected the mood of the time:

Tonight we meet to honour the voluntary laymen in our recreational program. In this rather materialistic and self-centered society, in which we live, service to one's fellowman is a characteristic of the highest order. The federation is such an organization of devoted and selfless individuals, dedicated to the service and betterment of mankind.

Today we are faced with the ever-increasing effects of automation, etc. on our lives. Leisure has become the property of all economic levels of our community. It is very easy to see why the federation now assumes, and will continue to assume, an ever-increasing role in the day to day welfare of our people.

That brochure also contained the words to the "Community League Song," sung to the tune of "Klondike Kate." The lyrics were:

Hey look us over, lend us your ear
Fresh out of money, mortgaged up to here,
Don't pass the buck boys we're full of cheer
We figure whenever you're down and out

The only way is up and out.
So we'll be around boys, just sign up here
Pay up your membership and be a volunteer.
Whatever you need you'll find it here
In your Community League.
So look out Edmonton, here we come!

During 1969, the community league movement scored another first—the creation of the first kindergarten program in Alberta. This occurred in the McLeod league under the able direction of Marion Spencer, who went on to provide a lifetime service to the league, area, and Edmonton.

During its September 1969 membership drive, the EFCL included ninety-six community leagues, which sought to again increase their overall membership. An EFCL brochure emphasized the value of league membership:

A league selling 650 memberships at $15.00 realizes $9,750 from this source. That's the member investment in the year's operation. The city's $500.00 grant amounts to roughly 4% of the league's total revenue of $10,250. Let's not kid ourselves into thinking that memberships aren't important.

With grants either scarce or limited in amount, the financial pressure on the leagues was truly dependent on membership revenue. Therefore, year after year there was a major media blitz during the September membership drive.

In July 1973, the EFCL received a $20,000 operating grant to hire a full-time director. Alderman Ron Hayter proposed the motion for the grant, which passed with a 6 to 5 vote. It was $10,000 less than requested by the EFCL; however, it was significantly higher than the $9,000 grant provided by the city to the federation in 1972. Similarly, the operating grants available to the leagues were increased by $100 to a maximum of $600. Shortly thereafter, Alderman Hayter was again in the news (reported in the November 14 *Edmonton Journal*) to recommend that any low-income family could turn to the city to secure a free league membership. The matter was defeated because, as alderman Cec Purves noted, "there'll be too many abuses probably."

A member of the Women's Auxiliary Air Force (WAAF) in Britain during World War II, Marion Spencer immigrated to Canada in 1948. After moving around Canada, in 1969 the Spencer family relocated to Edmonton, where Marion again became active in community life to provide decades of voluntary service. In the late 1960s, she became an original member of the McLeod Community League and served as its district commissioner for Girl Guides and Brownies. In 1969, she helped form the McLeod Kindergarten, which was the first such program in Alberta. She was involved in the formation of the Steele Heights Music Association and helped with a number of projects with M. E. Lazerte High School's parent association, including the creation of a school police officer post and the relocation of the public library.

For over twenty years, Spencer served on the executive of Area Council 17, where she was involved in countless projects from transportation, zoning, and planning to Christmas hamper delivery, recreation facility establishment, and bingo. In 1989, she assumed the position of chair of the Advisory Board for Medical Facilities in North Edmonton, which after ten years of community work led to the establishment of a community health centre in the area. Another of her major contributions resulted in financial support from the Rotary Club and the city for the construction of a water park in the area.

Spencer received much recognition for her selfless contribution to Edmonton and to other cities in which she lived. She received numerous awards from the EFCL including the Volunteer of the Year award (1996), a lifetime membership in Area Council 17, the Spirit of Edmonton award, Salute of Excellence award (1997), Canada 125th Anniversary commemorative medal, and the Northeast Rotary Club Integrity award (1996). In addition, she was nominated for the YWCA Tribute to Women award.

In April 1974, Arlene Meldrum became the first woman elected as EFCL president, replacing Murray Hawkins. She was a long-time volunteer and had made significant contributions to the EFCL figure skating program. Later that year saw the creation of "community councils," which had their origin in the two school boards. The idea was to establish community-focused committees that would guide the use of school facilities after the normal school period. These committees or councils were to have significant school-focused representation—trustees, representatives of administration, principals, and teachers—as well as representatives of the public. The latter group included the city (especially Parks and Recreation) and the EFCL as representative of the leagues. In time, these councils helped usher in the Joint Use Agreement, which is still in force today, to regulate the use of schools during the after-school period.

By 1977, however, the federation's relationship with the city had soured to a point of concern. A January 18 report titled *The Relationship Between the City and the Corporation of the City of Edmonton* expressed concern about the city's treatment of the leagues, noting that "from the vantage point of the Community Leagues their working relationships with the city are not working. Community leagues are excluded from procedural activities and collaboration is, at best, strained." It added that the leagues felt they "are not recognized as legitimate community representatives. Volunteers are being frustrated; their energies are subverted; and project costs are being increased by the breakdown of the partnership."

Under the leadership of President Don Eastcott, the federation pressed the city to allow the leagues a greater role in planning processes involving or affecting their respective area. Quoted in the *West Edmonton Examiner* on April 12, 1978, Eastcott noted, "The community leagues must realize that their responsibility is to the whole community." He added, "There is a popular trend in this city for citizen participation and citizen involvement [and] it is naïve to think the community leagues should exist only for hockey programs." In short, he advocated a more direct and active role for the leagues in the numerous planning issues that affected their current lives with lingering effects into their future. In fact, he was speaking for the era, as the leagues and their area councils were demanding more and more say in the development of their area. Countless examples illustrate the point. Here are some of the highlights.

Arlene Meldrum's life-long voluntary contribution to Edmonton was modelled on her mother's extensive commitment through the Imperial Order of the Daughters of the Empire (IODE) during World War II. Meldrum graduated from the University of Alberta, where she served as president of the Pi Beta Phi sorority. After graduation, she too joined IODE, a membership she held for many years.

Meldrum's involvement with the community league movement started in 1951, when she began to teach figure skating at various leagues. As her involvement grew, she joined the EFCL board as chair of its figure skating committee (1964–68). During that time, the program grew from 600 to over 6,000 and spawned numerous citywide shows and competitions. With increasing popularity and the need for additional coaches, Meldrum joined others to produce and deliver a coaches' training program. Then, to meet the growing need of men wishing to improve their skating, Meldrum helped develop a "power skating" program, delivered through a number of leagues across Edmonton.

Meldrum continued to serve on the EFCL board. She resigned in 1971, but returned to serve as EFCL president from 1972 to 1974. She represented the EFCL on the Parks and Recreation Board (1976–79) and on the management team that organized the Mayor's Neighbourhood Planning Conference. In 1978, she was appointed to the Mayor's Ad Hoc Committee on Citizen Participation, and she served on the Edmonton steering committee for the International Women's Year.

In 1995, Meldrum was appointed to a steering committee tasked with making the community a better place for seniors. She helped develop the Senior Friendly program that became a flagship of the Alberta Council on Aging, which spread the program throughout Alberta. By 1999, the program had gained national and international exposure.

Her many other voluntary services included: member of the Boys and Girls Club board, member of the Volunteer Manpower Committee of the 1978 Commonwealth Games Foundation, member of the YWCA Committee on Voluntarism, member of the Edmonton Association of Continuing Education and Recreation, chairperson of the Salary Review Committee (for mayor and aldermen), guide chairperson for the 1983 Universiade, member of the Grant McEwan College Volunteer Management Advisory Board (1982–83), member of the University of Alberta Senate (1984–90), volunteer organizer for the 1993 World Dinosaur Tour (1991–93), and member of the EFCL Revitalization Task Force (1997–99). Meldrum was the originator and prime mover of the Garbage Fairs (the first of which was held in her community), and she served on its 2004 steering committee.

Area 13[5] formed in 1968 with a budget of $59, yet it managed to establish the Hardisty Junior High Drop-in Centre, the Fulton arena and swimming pool, a community referral service, Open Door, and a mass blood-pressure screening in the neighbourhood. In 1975, Sheila McKay, the Area 13 president (who later became a city councillor and a member of the Capital Region Health Board), continued a three-year struggle to establish a community health-care centre in southeast Edmonton. In January 1975, she approached city council with a request for permission and annual funding (approximately $16,000) to hire a planner to look at better coordinating the city's helping agencies. The St. John's Ambulance *Edmonton Report* quoted her on January 27, 1975, saying, "Though there are at least 800 'helping agencies' in the city (one for every 500 citizens), help is hard to find in the face of 'numerous bureaucracies, reams of red tape and confusion'." A few years later Area 13 was again involved in a lengthy struggle, this time to get police patrols into the river valley parkway and to develop the area.

Three years later, Area Council 7 fought what it perceived to be an increase in utility billing to the leagues through a change of power meters from usage to demand. The new meter system billed users not on their monthly usage, but rather set a monthly rate based on their highest consumption in any billing period. This system penalized the leagues for their overly high power usage during the winter (for rink lighting and community hall usage) versus the low usage during the rest of the year. Area 7 was also embroiled in a long battle to secure more ice time for its programs from the ice-booking committee, which involved city representatives.

Area Council 1 in the northeast tackled the growing need for better north-south transportation routes in their area. Area Council 17, also in the north, tackled a broad range of local programs including the creation of a hospital. It also established and conducted a course for volunteer development. Area Council 14 in Mill Woods fought for a medical facility on 66th Street, which eventually became the site of the Grey Nuns Hospital, a regional care facility .

The late 1970s and 1980s increasingly involved individual leagues, area councils, and the federation in zoning and other developmental issues. It seems that citizen input, through the community league movement, helped review and influence every aspect of Edmonton's growing life. During 1978, Mayor Cec Purves held a number of neighbourhood conferences to identify existing issues and needs. In response, the federation compiled a 500-page report, which collected the league recommendations generated at these conferences. The EFCL presented the report to the mayor and council in early November. It received positive feedback and the assurance of Mayor and Alderman Lois Campbell, chair of the Public Affairs Committee, that they would routinely return to the public for policy and planning input.

A dominant theme of the report was the issue of citizen participation in the decision-making process. It recommended a thorough examination of the municipal government, the revision of the ward system (ensuring that aldermen live within their wards), establishment of an information ombudsman, creation of community liaison committees, development of information centres, passage of a bylaw to ensure citizen involvement in traffic and transportation planning, better planning and location of parkland, passage of a neighbourhood bill of rights, and much more.

While area councils and leagues were intended to work cooperatively, in 1979 they were pitted against each other in a battle over the Edmonton Rendering Company plant. Located in Edmonton's northeast on 61st Street at 129th Avenue, it needed to move. The city wanted to relocate it to a 2-hectare (5-acre) lot in the southeast, at 38th Street and 74th Avenue, but the folks in south Edmonton accused the city of treating them as either stupid or second-class citizens by dumping a plant so disliked by their northern neighbours. The battle became a hot potato for the city and the province. It was eventually resolved when the plant was relocated outside the city limits, in Strathcona

County. The process and its outcome illustrated the growing political involvement and intensity of league volunteers. Positive outcomes of the situation included the development of guidelines for the minimum distance that such plants should be from residential areas and the establishment of environmental controls.

During that year, three area councils—1, 2, and 17—joined forces to provide input on the selection of a site for a new hospital in their area. That relationship has withstood the test of time, and continues today. It has produced concerted community effort on many beneficial projects including transportation routes, school construction, zoning, and other community-planning or development issues.

One by one, the area councils and the federation's 118 community leagues created a flood of citizen input, which in turn created a concern for the EFCL. In May 1979, the federation approached city council with a request to establish a committee that would deal with the leagues' input on neighbourhood issues. The proposed committee structure consisted of representatives from the Parks and Recreation Department, the Parks and Recreation Advisory Board, and the EFCL. Its recommended mandate was to cooperate with city departments involved in the community and work out resolutions for consideration by city council.

In the summer of 1979, the federation asked to be "recognized" by city council as the formal voice on community issues. This request created much debate within and outside city hall. Don Wangas, in his "City Beat" column (Summer 1979), noted a dilemma for city council, but one of its own making. "Council has only itself to blame ... . Many mistakes have been made by councils past and present in dealing with the community at large. Numerous decisions which directly affect citizens have been made without their input. When citizens are asked for their views on matters concerning them it is too often done after the fact—when the important decisions have already been made." The basis of the federation's request was the desire to have a workable mechanism that would allow citizen input through the leagues before the city decided matters relating to development.

At its September 27 meeting, the federation formally gave its civic committee a clear mandate to enter the political arena. The vice-president of civic affairs, Don Williams, moved to authorize the eight-strong civic affairs committee to liaise with all levels of government (and other agencies) to facilitate citizen coordination, as outlined in the Mayor's Neighbourhood Planning Conference Task Force report. The motion passed, with the understanding that there was an element of urgency to the task and that the need for friendly relations with other groups did not require marrying league programs with those provided by external agencies.

A small example of the growing "citizen power" occurred in July 1979 at the Hardisty Community League and resulted in the overturning of a city decision in favour of the league residents. The matter related to pedestrian safety at the intersection of 65th Street and 106th Avenue, and involved a crossing extensively used by schoolchildren. The league and its area council realized that the city traffic and engineering department was set to establish flashing lights at one of three crossings in the area. In the league's opinion, inaccurate facts resulted in a poor decision that had placed the lights at the wrong intersection. A number of league volunteers set out to count the pedestrians using each of the three crossings and proved that their data was more accurate than the city's. The city believed the new findings to be accurate and moved the lights to the "correct" intersection—the one with the highest amount of pedestrian traffic.

Another interesting twist of community involvement related to the Calder Action Committee (CAC), which wanted to establish a league-owned and -operated business, with profits channelled to league programs. Jan Reimer (who later became mayor of Edmonton) represented the CAC and distributed a questionnaire to all Calder residents seeking their interest in and ideas for this corporation. The questionnaire received a strong response rate (30%) and raised a number of ideas. These included forming a consulting firm on matters involving citizen participation in municipal matters, a furniture recycling shop, and a food co-op for Calder-grown produce. Though similar ventures had worked in the United States and in Nova Scotia, the idea did not take root in Edmonton.

In any case, by the late 1970s and early 1980s the presence of the area councils was a reality of community life, even for the politicians of the day. The *North Edmonton Examiner* reported, on October 3, 1979, that at a meeting in Area 17, those in attendance heard that "the role of Area Councils will expand and change in the future." The meeting speakers were none other than Alderman Betty Hewes (later to become a provincial MLA), EFCL past president Arlene Meldrum, and Area Council 17 President Pat Wright.

Hewes challenged the area councils to concentrate on "social action" and leave the administrative functions to city staff. She observed that area councils "can work, and work extremely well, as long as they are not in the business of managing delivery services (which should remain in the government domain)." Meldrum emphasized that the EFCL had broadened its perception of area councils and that these councils comprised other agencies—church groups, schools, and community agencies—in addition to the leagues. However, she warned that the leagues continue to be pushed "to play a larger role than just recreation." Wright noted that the councils existed to serve a larger set of needs than just recreation, and emphasized that the purpose of the meeting was to identify "what function area councils should serve in the eye of the community residents." These three perspectives help explain the rift that grew between the federation and its area councils.

However, by 1980, there were signals that some area councils were headed for trouble. The greatest signs of looming danger appeared in the low attendance at the council meetings. In fact, some of the councils were on the edge of folding. Others did fold or simply did not get off the ground. Decades later, only a handful remain to continue their community-related service. (For details on the current area councils, see Appendix 2 "About the Area Councils.")

During 1980, the EFCL gained much-deserved (and needed) political recognition from city council, in the form of Policy C110—a resolution approved by the public affairs committee of city council that made the EFCL an effective arm of the local government.[6] According to the February 6, 1980, *South Edmonton Examiner*, the resolution recommended that the city:

- recognize each community league as a desirable vehicle for the provision of services which benefit the residents of the neighbourhood and the city
- view the community league structure as a useful mechanism for debate of area concerns and presentation of views and recommendations to council
- believe that participation in community league activity is a desirable element in a democracy which seeks to place decision making for appropriate activities at the neighbourhood level

- recognize the role the community league structure plays in educating and training citizens in government and in providing opportunities for citizens to volunteer their services to the community
- support the EFCL as the representative and coordinating body of Edmonton's community leagues
- direct the administration to give support to community leagues so the resources of citizens and the administration can work productively for the benefit of the city as a whole

In the same issue of the *Examiner*, EFCL president Clint Budd said: "From my view point it's a gateway to council ... . By rights we should never again get the question: 'who in the hell are you and who says you speak for the people in your neighbourhood'." The policy was a monumental milestone for the community league movement. By May, city administration and the council's public affairs committee had approved a list of the EFCL's recommendations, generated through extensive consultation with the leagues, which greatly advanced the process. The *Southwest Edmonton Examiner* reported the following recommendations:

- A contact person be available in each city department having dealings with community leagues. [However, by the mid-1990s this boiled down to only one person at the Parks and Recreation Department.]
- A full-time liaison officer be appointed by the city as a permanent link between the federation and the city.
- The federation be given representation on the joint planning committee.
- Community leagues be recognized as a vehicle for organized public participation.
- The city prepare a "citizens guide" to city hall.
- Informal meetings be continued between the federation executive and city council members.
- Annual operating grants to the federation and individual leagues be reviewed on a three-year basis, effective 1981.

By July 1980, city council had once again expanded its recognition of the EFCL and the leagues as the best mechanism for allowing citizen input into the planning or developmental issues at local level. Accordingly, council designated the leagues as the sole community group to receive formal notification of development applications for projects in their area or close enough to affect them. Alderman Ed Kennedy suggested that community planning groups, which have traditionally been active in this area, should be notified as well. Councillors Betty Hewes and Percy Wickman supported his proposal, while councillors Ron Hayter, Olivia Butti, and Bill Chmiliar adamantly opposed it. In the end, the honour remained the leagues' alone. (Area councils lacked the same opportunity to be included in the notification process and in September 2003 successfully challenged the matter.)

By 1983, the EFCL boasted of a membership that included 134 community leagues across the city. These leagues, their area councils, and the EFCL executive were involved in seemingly all facets of the community, advocating for a better life for Edmonton's residents. League volunteers dealt with numerous issues, including protection of the river valley and other designated recreation spaces, protection of schools from closing, establishment of new hospital or care facilities, establishment of laws against the carrying of firearms by minors, creation of arcade controls, reversal of bingo and casino opportunities (set by the province), funding for the leagues, and much more. These were times of mutual support between the EFCL and the city, though occasional spats required much effort to mend the damage and move on. Internally too, the EFCL had sustained a great deal of cooperation among its many components—the leagues, area councils, and the board, which continued to grow in size.

By August 1983, the first signs appeared indicating a trend that would grow from a trickle to a flood—the partnership of city departments with volunteer agencies, most often the community leagues. In his August 1 column in the *Edmonton Sun*, Allan Bolstad (who served in the 1990s as city councillor) proclaimed, "Hundreds of city parks are up for adoption, and you may be the park-parent the city is looking for... . The parks and recreation department is stepping up its recruitment of citizens to help develop, manage or maintain city parks."

The root of the problem, according to planning director Wanda Wetterberg, was the lack of sufficient funds to undertake all the department's projects. Many instances already existed where the community had stepped up to the plate to do its share—the north-end sports teams that helped line and maintain ball diamonds and soccer fields, the donation of $10,000 by Area Council 2 for swimming pool equipment, the five leagues in Mill Woods that had constructed their own playgrounds, and many more. In short, it was an effort to push the limit on the capacity of the volunteer sector to provide services that more often fell under the realm of the municipal government. Over time, all of the area councils contributed to the city's effort.

That year, an EFCL crime reduction initiative, Neighbourhood Watch—a joint initiative between the EFCL and the Edmonton Police Department (later renamed the Edmonton Police Service)—began to pay off. The year began with fifty communities involved in the monitoring and protection of their league area. The program proved a tremendous success. In time, the growing number of participants led to its evolution into its current structure as an independent organization.

In May 1984, the EFCL received the 7-Eleven Police Week award for its crime prevention effort. Edmonton Police Service Sergeant Joe Dumonceaux, who was also the EFCL president, accepted the award on behalf of the federation and noted that 72 of 136 leagues were already participating in the program. The July 23 issue of the *Edmonton Examiner* reported that support for Neighbourhood Watch was growing rapidly, with over 3,300 block captains covering more than 26,000 homes across the city. By February 1985, the number of participating leagues had grown to 100, representing over 40,000 houses.

Other community initiatives, such as Block Parents and the Community Police Radio Network (CPRN), flourished too. Collectively they supported the city's crime prevention program, which in 1985 became the third most successful such program in North America. Police Chief Robert Lunney observed in the March 18 *Edmonton Examiner* that "the secret of our success is the community. The community has a team spirit. It's involved in all facets of the program." With more than 31 leagues contributing to the program, it raised over $35,000. Additionally, 11,464 tips resulted in 434 arrests in the area, the recovery of over $1.5 million in stolen property, and the seizure of more than $6 million worth of drugs.

During 1984, the EFCL also set up a special committee to prepare a position paper on pornography and prostitution. Chaired by past President Arlene

Meldrum, the committee developed a brief designed to provide information, get people thinking, and propose solutions to the problem. The brief, presented by the committee to the EFCL board in April of that year, expressed concerns about the impact that the media, most notably television, was having on the attitudes of the public.

The next year began with upbeat notes for the EFCL. In 1985, the federation established its first youth chairman when it appointed 24-year-old Doris Woodman to the job of coordinating and promoting youth activities at league level. The initiative was part of the United Nations International Youth Year. The February 25 issue of the *Edmonton Examiner* reported that Woodman intended to seek ideas for action from those she wanted to serve—the youth across the city. She invited anyone with ideas for youth programs to contact her.

Another positive action by the EFCL was the completion of its long negotiation on behalf of the leagues with the city regarding the Standard Lease Agreement, which guided the league's use of city lands or facilities. It took much time and effort, involving various lawyers on both sides, to develop a framework that was adaptable to the diverse needs of all community leagues. Before ratification in early 1985, the EFCL sought feedback from all leagues. The final agreement passed the test of time. Although it has evolved, it continues to guide the city–league relationship today.

Another success story was the EFCL's biweekly column in the *Edmonton Examiner*. Inaugurated on January 28, 1985, and written by Wayne Taylor, chair of the EFCL publicity committee, the column provided information on a wide variety of community-related issues and activities.

Financial good news also came early in the year. The leagues started to experience greater and greater access to grant opportunities and financial support. Grants became available from all orders of government and facilitated a variety of projects including the construction or renovations of community halls, playgrounds, parks, and ice rinks. One such grant was the Community Recreation-Cultural (CRC) grant, which on April 1 replaced the Major Cultural-Recreation Facility Development (MCR) program. The beauty of the new program was that it ensured a minimum of 50 percent of the province's recreation-grant funds be allocated to community groups—a significant increase from the 30-percent limit under the MCR. In the meanwhile, numerous Canada Works projects were also approved, many targeted toward the needs of community leagues. Under this arrangement, in February the EFCL received nearly $17,000 to produce a catalogue of common products and suppliers for all leagues.

Amidst all this excitement and flurry of activity, Clareview area residents had excitement of their own: cats, and more cats! An *Edmonton Examiner* report on February 25, 1985, detailed the infestation of the area with unruly felines. "We're being bombarded with calls from people complaining about cats," said Don Couts, a director of the Bannerman Community League. "The cats are clawing up fences, scratching up the hoods of cars and causing all sorts of damage." There was talk of poisoning or shooting the cats. However, the leagues involved discouraged this option. The suggestion to take the stray cats to the SPCA also quickly disappeared, discouraged by the SPCA representative's comments that the act would constitute theft. According to the law of the day, citizens could only return trapped cats to their owners. City officials acknowledged the problem, but noted the current bylaw did not deal with the situation. In 1984 alone, the SPCA sheltered more than 5,600 stray cats. The situation was remedied a number of years later.

In November 1985, an eleven-person Mayor's Task Force chaired by Alderman Percy Wickman recommended the creation of a "culture commission" that would disburse funds for cultural and ethnic groups. (This task force reflected the introduction of "ethnopolitics" during the fall Conservative Party leadership race, during which the soon-to-be-elected-premier Don Getty visibly courted minority groups and their leaders.) The idea had much support from Mayor Lawrence Decore, but created tremendous controversy within council and across the city's community groups.

The task force recommended that a sixteen-member culture commission be created, with equal representation from Edmonton's diverse cultural and ethnic groups. After a heated debate, which included a threat of resignation by Wickman, city council agreed to accept the idea in principle. A compromise solution raised by Alderman Jan Reimer established a six-member implementation committee that would study the matter further. That committee included one representative each from council, city administration, the Edmonton Parks, Recreation and Culture Advisory Committee, the Edmonton Culture Caucus, the Edmonton Professional Arts Caucus, and the EFCL.

> Edmonton's amazing population growth in the 1970s came mostly
> from immigration, relocation from rural areas, and movement of
> Canadians from less prosperous provinces. By the mid 1970s,
> Alberta's population reflected a diverse ethnicity, including 45
> percent British, 13 percent Ukrainian, 12 percent German, 7 percent
> French, and 5 percent Scandinavian. A large portion (65%) of
> Edmonton's population was under 35 years of age.

The matter raised hackles on both sides of the debate, which centred on the control of city grant monies as well as what constituted "culture." The EFCL was fighting what it perceived as a threat to its funding. On January 27, 1986, the federation boycotted the implementation committee's meeting, because it rejected the intended administration of the culture policy. However, on March 31, the EFCL rejoined the discussion to express its reservations. It identified four major objections:

- the culture commission's lack of accountability to city council
- the recommended guaranteed funding component (the EFCL wanted annual funding requests)
- the negative or unpredictable effect that funding for the proposed culture commission would have on funding for community leagues
- the likely elimination of the current CRC grants from the authority of the Edmonton Parks and Recreation Culture Advisory Board

The implementation committee struggled with the format of the culture commission and experimented with a variety of possibilities regarding membership, size, and arrangements. At one point, a fifteen-member board was recommended, including three representatives each from the Professional Arts Council, the Multicultural Society, and the EFCL, one member each from the public school board and the separate school board, and four members appointed by city council.

This raised the hackles of Alderman Ron Hayter. Quoted in the September 12, 1986, issue of the *Examiner*, he noted his objection: "I do not believe that any civic board, or committee, should be dominated by designated members representing vested groups." Councillors Terry Cavanagh and Ken Kozak supported him. Nevertheless, when the bylaw passed on September 23, the size and composition of the culture commission remained unchanged.

A few months before, in early June, the EFCL went through its own soul-searching and reorganization. It decided to double the term of its executive positions including president, vice-president civic, vice-president external affairs, secretary-treasurer, and three directors at large. According to EFCL President Brian Sugiyama, the schedule involved annual elections for half the positions to provide gradual turnover and continuity at the executive level. Sugiyama hoped that this arrangement would create stability for the board as a whole.

Also in June, the EFCL published a book outlining the incredible history of all its leagues. The book—*Volunteers: The History of the Community League Movement in Edmonton*, by 31-year-old Michael Wanchuk and 30-year-old Vaughn Bowler— gave an overview of the federation as well as a brief history of each of its existing leagues.

Sugiyama resigned on December 15, 1986 (for a job offer in Ladysmith, B.C.), relinquishing to his successor, John Bracegirdle, a major battle with the city over the threat of the EFCL losing its traditional municipal funding source to the growing political support for the arts and ethno-cultural groups. Mayor Decore and two aldermen—Lance White and Julian Kinisky—were pushing for increased funding for the culture commission.

In his January 27 column in the *Edmonton Sun*, Allan Bolstad (soon to become Alderman Bolstad) noted, "It's no secret [that] arts and ethno-culture groups are moving in on the federation's primary source of funding. The EFCL will have to get in and fight if it doesn't want to be pushed around." He added that "Sugiyama says he can see the writing on the wall and he intends to pass the word on to Bracegirdle. 'We're going to have to take some tough stands'."

A budding politician, Bracegirdle was the right person for the job. During the municipal election in October 1986, he placed sixth in Ward 6. His extensive experience in the community league movement included serving as chair of the Mill Woods Presidents' Council, member of the Edmonton Parks, Recreation and Cultural Advisory Committee, and member of a committee that looked at strengthening the area councils.

John Bracegirdle grew up in Edmonton and devoted much volunteer time to its welfare. He served in numerous organizations and in various roles within each, including as president of the Edmonton Klondike Days Association, president of the EFCL, president of the Mill Woods Cultural and Recreational Facilities Association (MCARFA), president of the Mill Woods Presidents' Council, president of the Southwood Community League, director with the Boys Scouts of Canada, and a volunteer with both the Universiade Games and the Commonwealth Games.

Bracegirdle has also been actively involved in local politics. In 1986 and again in 1989, he ran for city council. He also served in various posts on a number of provincial and federal Progressive Conservative Party associations.

Municipal budget cuts in April 1987 began to bring Sugiyama's message home. Among those affected was the Castle Downs Twin Arena complex. According to city officials, the cuts resulted from provincial cutbacks, which led to a reduction of $1.1 million in Community Recreation-Cultural (CRC) current funding and an anticipated $11.6-million funding cut for capital development over the remaining four years in the CRC grant program. The ward's two councillors, Jan Reimer and Ron Hayter, had pledged their commitment to the facility and expressed their anger at its potential loss. "That facility is needed and it's a top priority for the community," they stated in the April 25 *Edmonton Journal*.

As time went on, the EFCL became more and more political. In late 1988, the federation opposed the expenditure of public funds for the Commonwealth Stadium, supported its leagues in north and south Edmonton against the creation of a landfill site in their areas, and encouraged the city to develop alternative solutions to the landfill (in favour of recycling programs). The federation and its leagues continued to provide a variety of programs and services, which continued to increase in both complexity and number.

One such program was the Youth Awards—the brainchild of June Cavanagh. She came up with the idea that the federation needed to recognize the talent, commitment, and effort of youth in making the city a better place to live.

Recipients of the EFCL Youth Award, circa 1992.
EFCL collection.

Cavanagh worked diligently for many years to ensure that the program had sufficient sponsors and was attractive to youth from the various leagues. For many years, the Youth Awards recognized dedicated young people who grew up to become leaders and major contributors within their communities.

However, all of this effort by the federation came at a tremendous cost to the organization and its volunteers, who hoped to continue delivering more and more programs, though they were under mounting pressure to raise the necessary funds. The *Strathcona Free Press* noted, on September 1, 1988, that "there is no money available for playgrounds in new districts, so communities are being forced to build them on their own." Bracegirdle was quoted as saying, "Originally, there was supposed to be a 50–50 relationship between the [City and the EFCL], but the City is now taking on a 'big brother' role that many communities resent." Additionally, he noted, "rather than see a program fail, individual community members tend to overwork themselves and burn out."

The warning signs were clearly visible. The future of the federation and its leagues was becoming more complex and less financially friendly, and volunteers were becoming a scarce commodity. During this period, many of

June Carol Cavanagh is a long-time community volunteer, a tremendous fundraiser, and a fierce advocate of the community league movement and many other community-based agencies. She has devoted decades of her time, talent, and care to enhancing the quality of life in Edmonton. Cavanagh has been involved in countless organizations, projects, and activities, including the EFCL, Northlands Park, Edmonton Immigrant Service Association, Heart Fund, and Daffodil Day, plus she has served on numerous boards, from the Alberta Ballet and Fort Edmonton Park to the Kidney Foundation and the United Way.

Cavanagh's indefatigable fundraising efforts benefited the 1983 Commonwealth Games, the 1983 Universiade, the Northeast Edmonton Medical Centre, the Salvation Army, various youth centres, and countless other projects and programs. During 1980–83, she also served as alderman in Ward 3. Cavanagh has been nominated for and received numerous awards. These included a Salute to Excellence Award citation (1991), a nomination for the 1991 Woman's Award, a Distinguished Service Award from the Canadian Association of Exhibitors (1993), and a thirty-year pin for volunteer service at Northlands (1994). She is married to long-time Ward 6 city councillor Terry Cavanagh, who twice served as Edmonton's mayor.

the federation-initiated sport programs splintered off and became independent associations. Additionally, the creation and evolution of the Edmonton Sports Council encouraged the federation and its leagues to refocus on recreational activities versus sports. Yet despite the many changes to its operation, the federation marched onward, toward meeting greater demands—with its volunteers once again shouldering the burden.

Many persons have the wrong idea about what
constitutes true happiness. It is not attained
through self-gratification but through fidelity
to a worthy purpose.

— HELEN KELLER

Behind an able man,
there are always other able men.

— CHINESE PROVERB

6

Picking Up
the Slack,
Again

1988–1998

A community is too heavy
for anyone to carry alone.

— DEUTERONOMY RABBAH

THE LATE 1970S WERE TOUGH FOR THOSE IN EASTERN CANADA. High
unemployment, astronomical interest rates (as high as 24%), and
runaway inflation created financial and social havoc. In Alberta, the continued
success and growth of the province's oil-based industry initially softened the
economic hardships. Nevertheless, by 1982 the recession had hit Alberta and
caused a tremendous stir, partly because of its impact and partly because of the
perception that it was Ottawa-induced and unnecessary.

The West, and especially Alberta, deemed the National Energy Program
(NEP) initiated by the Pierre Trudeau government to be a major culprit in the
economic downturn of the 1980s.[1] The NEP developed after the 1980 federal
election, in which the Liberals swept into power even before the counting of the
votes in the West. In a meeting between Prime Minister Trudeau and Premier
Peter Lougheed following the election, Lougheed offered to sell Alberta's oil at
75 percent of the world price to Canadian consumers.

The offer was rejected, and on October 28, 1982, federal finance minister
Allan MacEachen presented his budget, which relied heavily on a reduced price
for Alberta oil and gas. Under a revised formula and a new federal tax, Ottawa

intended to buy Alberta's oil at seventeen dollars per barrel when it was selling in the world markets for forty dollars per barrel. Alberta's war with Ottawa began, and it immediately produced casualties. Within two months, around sixty oil and gas drilling rigs left Alberta for the United States. The sight of these rigs heading south was ominous for the provincial economy and its people.

Weak oil prices in the early 1980s further aggravated the situation and dampened the provincial economy. Things went steadily from bad to worse. Unemployment rose from an average of 4 percent in early 1981 to 12 percent by the end of that year.

With an unemployment rate of 14 percent in early 1983, Calgary and Edmonton suffered significantly more than the rest of the province. The impact existed in all sectors of the economy and along all organizational levels. During 1982, Alberta's economy shrank by 5 percent. The construction sector lost 25 percent of its jobs, the manufacturing sector shed a third of its employees, and over 30 percent of forest industry workers received layoff notices or had their work time reduced. By the fall of 1983, unemployment had nearly tripled, affecting 68,000 Albertans.

Predictably, the deterioration of Alberta's economic conditions reversed a long-time trend of migration into the province, and most notably into its two largest cities—Edmonton and Calgary. In 1981, Alberta showed a quarterly gain of 25,000 people, but by the last quarter of 1982 the province had a net loss of 3,400 people. The population loss was devastating, if for no other reason than its uniqueness. This was the first population loss for Alberta since 1945, and the first for Calgary in one hundred years! The population drain, coupled with loss of income and anxiety over the economy, affected the housing market, which in the mid-1980s took a nosedive from which it wouldn't recover until the late 1990s. By early 1984, the average upscale house had lost nearly 40 percent of its value.

All this turmoil festered and spilled into the political arena, where Ottawa, the federal Liberal Party, Energy Minister Marc Lalonde, Finance Minister Allan MacEachen, and Prime Minister Pierre Trudeau became the primary villains for conservative-leaning Alberta. The public and the media vilified Alberta's premier, Peter Lougheed, and many others, accusing them of selling out the West and Alberta. Some saw this "treachery" as sufficient cause for drastic action. "Separation!" rose like a battle cry, raised by a number of individuals from different political backgrounds or interests. They included such colourful characters as Doug Christie (Western Canada Concept), Elmer Knutson (West-Fed Association), Gordon Kesler, Al Maygard, and Howard Thompson (Western Canada Concept).

The NEP-generated recession of 1981–82 seemed to be quickly over. This impression developed during 1983 and 1985, which involved a slight recovery of the economy with a 4.5 percent increase in Alberta's gross domestic product. However, in 1986, Alberta's economy imploded. Layoffs in the oil patch began almost immediately. The price of North Sea oil plummeted in February 1986 to US$18 per barrel, further reducing the "Alberta Advantage." Forests of FOR SALE and CLOSING-OUT SALE signs littered the landscape, especially in Edmonton and Calgary, where conditions deteriorated rapidly. In March, Edmonton had the dubious honour of having the highest unemployment rate (11.1%) in Alberta, and by fall, there were 24,000 Edmonton residents on welfare. A great number of those unemployed or on welfare left for greener pastures in other provinces, notably Ontario.

By mid-June, oil prices hit another low—US$15 per barrel—and the future continued to look even gloomier. In August, provincial treasurer Dick Johnston introduced legislation that permitted Alberta to borrow extensively (as much as $5.5 billion) to fund its 1986–87 budget. The oil industry and other businesses also began to borrow heavily, trim costs significantly, or more often do both. The survival-mode behaviour at corporate level further increased the ranks of the unemployed and reduced disposable income. A slim bit of good news arrived in October 1986, when the federal government eliminated one of the last vestiges of the detested National Energy Program—the petroleum and gas revenue tax.

The economic outlook was bewildering at best. Even those who had lived through the Depression could not understand the chaos in Alberta's economy. Choices for those cast aside by the cuts and layoffs were few. Some left the province; some went on unemployment. According to Statistics Canada estimates published in January 1987, as many as 6,000 workers dropped from the workforce. Nearly 50,000 Edmonton residents were unemployed that month, representing 12.5 percent of its work force.

Predictably, the number of people (and families) on welfare, and their related expenses, rose dramatically. Then, as if by magic and not good management, the economic thunderstorm rapidly moved on. By June 1987, indicators pointed to better times ahead. By September, oil prices had risen to a steady US$20 per barrel and the unemployment rate in Edmonton had dropped to a low of 9.7 percent. In May 1989, Edmonton's unemployment rate reached 7.5 percent—the lowest level since 1981—bringing an influx of workers to Edmonton and reducing the city's apartment vacancy rate to 3.6 percent, its lowest level since 1982.

The economic downturn and its turnaround raised demands for diversification of Alberta's economy and reduced reliance on the oil and gas sector. This led to a variety of massive projects, many focused on the forest industry. First among them was the 1986 opening of the Millar Western Industries pulp mill in Whitecourt, north of Edmonton.

In the late 1980s and early 1990s[2], Edmonton's residents were spectators to a number of dramas that unfolded in the streets, in front of the Legislature Building, and in the media: the 1988 illegal walkout by the nurses' union; the violent and lengthy strike at Peter Pocklington's Gainers meat-packing plant in north Edmonton; and the collapse of the Edmonton-based Principal Group of companies headed by Donald Cormie.

This was in Premier Don Getty's era with its many diversification projects, which were extremely costly and left a legacy that lingers today. When elected in November 1985, the Getty government had inherited $12.6 billion in assets. In 1992, when Getty retired as premier, Alberta had a net debt of $3.9 billion.

The economic stresses had devastating impacts on the social infrastructure of the city. One indicator in the late 1980s was the rise in the local crime rate. Edmonton had the highest per-capita homicide rate among urban centres in Canada and gained the dubious title of "Canada's murder capital."

In 1992, partially in response to the alarming situation, the Edmonton Police Service introduced its "Community Policing" and prevention programs, which proved extremely useful. Within three years the city experienced an amazing 43-percent drop in its crime rate. (Community policing, which drew the attention of many other police departments across Canada and the United States, continues to evolve and entrench at the local level.)

The late 1980s and early 1990s saw a growing imbalance between Edmonton and Calgary, which led to the intensification of competition between the two cities on all fronts: economics, promotions, politics, and sports. The provincial government's downsizing of that period further tilted the balance in favour of Calgary. By 1994 Edmonton was losing 1,500 residents a year to Calgary, an exodus reflecting Calgary's growing strength as a corporate centre. A 1994 survey in the *Financial Post* revealed that of the eighty-two Fortune-500 companies that called Alberta home, twelve—with total assets of $10.2 billion—resided in Edmonton. By comparison, Calgary was home to sixty-seven companies—with total assets of around $80 billion.

Further aggravating the situation was the uneasy relationship between Edmonton's mayor, Jan Reimer, and elements of the local business community. Reimer, the city's first woman mayor and the daughter of a former NDP leader, had her allies among labour, environmental groups, and the public sector. Part of her legacy was the completion in 1992 of a new city hall, which opened on August 14 and received numerous awards for its design and construction technology. However, despite all Reimer's efforts, Edmonton kept losing its foothold in the economic competition with Calgary. The devastating results became worse in 1994 with the eruption of the "Klein Revolution," a term coined by *Edmonton Journal* columnist Marc Lisac.

In 1988, after years of Edmonton-bashing as Calgary's mayor, Ralph Klein entered provincial politics, won a seat as a Member of the Legislative Assembly (MLA), and moved to Edmonton to become minister of the environment. The leadership campaign that followed Premier Don Getty's resignation in 1992 was a close one, with Klein seen as the front-runner. In the end, he received 60 percent of the votes. Premier "Ralph" had a strong mandate within the party, which soon resulted in a political shuffle. One of the products of that shuffle was that Edmonton remained completely unrepresented on the provincial cabinet. A year later, following the provincial election, the Conservative Party and Klein had a strong mandate for action from the general electorate—fifty-one seats versus the Liberal Party's thirty-two, and none for the NDP. The election also cleared out a number of the Getty-era ministers and MLAs.

By then, Alberta's finance minister, Jim Dinning, had initiated an independent review of the province's finances through a financial review commission which, after determining that provincial finances were worse than anticipated, recommended significant cuts. The need to seriously rein in government expenditure soon led to every department being directed to cut 20 percent of its budget.

Additionally, a number of privatization initiatives were implemented, the most notable involving the province's 204 government-controlled liquor-sale outlets. The cuts affected everything including the basics—health, education, social services, and infrastructure.

In 1995, Bill Smith, who ran on a pro-business and pro-development platform, replaced Reimer as mayor. Dubbed "Booster Bill" by the *Edmonton Sun*, Smith set out to aggressively promote the city to anyone and everyone who would listen. His often-repeated statement about Edmonton being "the best city in the best province in the best country in the world" soon caught attention and became his trademark.

Smith's energetic approach, determination, and closer relationship to the ruling Conservative provincial government started to narrow the financial gap between Edmonton and Calgary. By the late 1990s, the economic differences between the two cities were less profound than in the previous decade. Part of that was thanks to the federal government's transfer in 1998 of more than 1,200 soldiers and their families to Edmonton, and the enhancements made to the local base.

Sports were often a hot topic of discussion in the 1990s and received much coverage by the media. Key among the teams closely monitored by fans and the media alike were the Edmonton Oilers and the Edmonton Eskimos. Each was involved in its own "Battle of Alberta"—fiercely fought competitions with rivals: the Calgary Flames and the Calgary Stampeders. The Oilers maintained their strong lead, winning numerous awards, including the coveted Stanley Cup on five occasions. (The Flames finally won their first and only Stanley Cup in 1989.) Edmonton also boasted of having No. 99—Wayne Gretzky.

Edmonton's residents supported many other sport programs and professional teams. For example, in 1996 Edmonton hosted the World Figure Skating Championships, the World Firefighter Games, and the LPGA du Maurier Classic. These events reflected the city's increasing status as a sophisticated and physically active community. Indeed, recreation and sports were gaining increasing interest among the city's residents.

Edmonton's population in 1988 was relatively young, with 74 percent of its residents being under forty-five. Its population had over $15.1 billion in disposable income and was extremely diverse, sustaining nearly 800 ethno-cultural organizations throughout the city. During the 1990s, perhaps because of the cuts in traditional employers—the public sector and the gas/oil industry—much effort went into developing economic diversification. By 1997,

Oil plants along Edmonton's eastern border with Strathcona County.
City of Edmonton Archives ET-14-87.

Edmonton had become the industrial heart of Alberta, producing nearly 45 percent of the province's value-added manufacturing and creating nearly $15 billion in goods. During that year, Edmonton's manufacturing-sector work-force increased by 8,000 to 50,600—a sign that the economy was recovering.

Edmonton's strong economic potential, competent workforce, and promising environment achieved repeated recognition. In 1993, Edmonton secured a rating as one of the top five cities in Canada for its business environment. (The city's economy received an honourable mention in 1992 and again in 1997.) In 1995, *Report on Business* magazine identified Edmonton as one of the top five "Smart Cities" in Canada. (A "Smart City" is defined as one that creates an environment that fosters creativity and knowledge-based business or research.)

By 1999, Edmonton's economy was doing well. Early that year, KPMG conducted a study that ranked the typical operating costs of medium-sized businesses. Edmonton was rated first with the lowest cost. Also that spring, a study by *Industry Week* identified Edmonton's workforce as being the most productive of all Canadian cities. In summer 1999, a report by the Conference Board of Canada ranked Edmonton's economy as the most diverse among

Canada's cities. (The report also provided a forecast of a strong growth—3.8%—for Edmonton in the following year.) At that time, the International Development Research Committee also named Edmonton as a "Smart City." It was a designation given to no other Canadian city and to only five other cities around the world.

Edmonton's population of 605,538 in 1990 grew to 624,000 by 1997.[3] Metropolitan Edmonton, which includes seventeen population centres and four rural counties, had a population of 870,000 and was the fifth largest centre in Canada. Its population demographics reflected a young population—with 62 percent younger than forty—and an equal balance between males and females in all age groups. Its geographical area increased to 700 square kilometres (270 square miles). Because two-thirds of the province's farming operations were located within the metropolitan Edmonton market area, the area remained important to Alberta's agriculture. The region also served as an important manufacturing and service centre for the area's agriculture activity. Edmonton was also judged important to a variety of sectors including forestry, manufacturing (adding about 40% of the $5-billion provincial output), construction, trade, financial institutions, and public administration.

Edmonton's growth affected a number of communities and satellite municipalities within a thirty-minute drive from downtown, including St. Albert, Sherwood Park, Fort Saskatchewan, Spruce Grove, Stony Plain, Devon, Beaumont, and Leduc.

In the dozen years from 1983 to 1995, Canadian air traffic grew rapidly, especially at the Calgary, Vancouver, and Winnipeg international airports. This was not the case at the Edmonton International Airport, where air traffic dropped by 6 percent. The situation brought the continued existence of Edmonton's two airports to a head. A civic referendum in late 1995 resulted in the consolidation of nearly all air passenger traffic at the international airport. The decision and subsequent action resulted in a sudden 2.5 percent increase in air traffic at the Edmonton International Airport, which outstripped the growth at all other city airports across Canada. In 1995, direct flights from Edmonton more than doubled, increasing from eighteen to forty destinations. Edmonton's international airport underwent a major and costly—$300 million—upgrade to expand its runways, parking, and terminal facilities.

The 1990s also saw a major refinement of the various festivals that run sequentially in Edmonton through the summer days. These sophisticated and entertaining events were typically free or at reasonable rates. Many of them have gained international recognition.

For example, when established in 1985 the Edmonton International Street Performers Festival was the first such event in North America. "The Works" is the largest visual arts festival in North America. The Northern Alberta Children's Festival, established in 1981, is the second oldest and the third largest children's festival in Canada. The ten-day Klondike Days celebration (or "K-Days") started in 1962; in 1997, it received its fourth Major Fair of the Year award from the Canadian Association of Fairs and Expositions. The Kiwanis Music Festival, established in 1908, is the oldest and one of the largest music festivals in Canada. The Heritage Festival, started in 1975, is often billed as the "largest one-site multicultural festival in the world." In 1999, the American Business Association designated the Heritage Festival as one of the top 100 events in North America. The Fringe Theatre Festival, which started in 1982, is the largest festival of alternative theatre in North America. The many other festivals involve a diversity of cultural and ethnic activities.[4]

Additionally, Edmonton's residents and visitors enjoy access to a wide variety of recreation and sports opportunities, many funded by the city. These include professional sports or tournaments (from local to international), parks, and recreation facilities. Edmonton's river valley—with its 25-kilometre (15-mile) park nicknamed "ribbon of green"—provides trails for bicycling, walking, or running from one end of the city to the other. Of Edmonton's 1997 budget of just over $972 million, almost $80.5 million went to parks and recreation.

The city residents required (and demanded) more recreational and sport opportunities than those provided by the city, and the community league movement continued its long-time effort to fill the void. The reward for this effort became apparent at tax time, when the city exempted the leagues from paying municipal property taxes. Even when new provincial rules forced the city to review its designation of organizations as free from municipal taxes, it continued to exempt the leagues. Under the new regulations, community leagues were the only agencies to have their municipal tax forgiven. This exemption was a much-needed break for the Edmonton Federation of Community Leagues (EFCL) and its leagues, which were staggering under the financial load placed upon them by reduced support from the public sector along with increasing expectations.

The 1990s were a particularly turbulent and trying time for the community league movement in Edmonton. The federation and its leagues went through an acrimonious relationship that almost imploded the EFCL due to its internal bickering. It was a tough period, felt more at federation level than by the individual leagues. In short, the various leagues across the city continued to do what they had done best for many decades—provide recreational and sport opportunities for the youth in their community and strive to enhance the quality of life in their respective league area, district, or across the city. During much of this decade, most league volunteers went about their business with little knowledge or regard for the infighting that was tearing the EFCL board limb from limb.

Those who lived through the experience described the period, the EFCL board, and its members in terms like "dysfunctional," "bloated," "egotistical," and "extremely political." Through the evolution of its programs and services, the EFCL board had grown to an unruly group that reached as many as forty-two members. Its membership reflected a collection of increasingly diverse agendas, often at odds with each other. Some openly opposed the EFCL's fundamental survival as the representative of the city's community leagues. Predictably, the board quickly became splintered by differences of ideology, policy direction, and management practices.

Key among these other interest groups were the area councils, which were gaining in strength, recognition, and the desire to be politically active. The subgroups or "camps" were entrenched in their intended course of action, and over time they became less tolerant of opposing views. The results were visibly devastating, and board meetings often involved insults, shouting matches, and personal attacks. Relations between the few staff members and key board members became strained and in one case led to a lawsuit over alleged defamation.

On October 3, 1997, the *Edmonton Examiner* reported that area council representatives were asking the city to audit the EFCL finances as far back as 1992. The call came in the context of a recently completed auditor's report, which criticized EFCL bookkeeping practices as "inadequate." The matter also came up at the federation's general meeting. On December 5, under the headline

An EFCL Board meeting chaired by EFCL President Ed Gibbons (center), circa 1996.
EFCL collection.

"EFCL Members Want Help To Stop Infighting," the *Edmonton Journal* reported
at length on the conflict. It quoted Mike McGowan, president of Southwood
Community League, as saying, "There appears to be a strong sense of personal
agendas, politicking, one-upmanship, bickering, infighting and general disrup-
tive behaviour that pervades the entire organization."

The article also reported that EFCL President Corky Meyer, who had earlier
resigned from the board, did so because of differing ideologies. She stated that
the divided board was comprised of those who believed in cost recovery and
wanted to charge the leagues for the services of the EFCL office, and those who
felt that the status quo (no charge-back) had to remain.

In fact, there was much more to the infighting than that, and it often came
down to personality conflicts. Former EFCL president Ed Gibbons (who later served
as a Liberal MLA and on city council) and treasurer Kevin Shopik were accused of
taking an unauthorized trip to Halifax in 1996, paid for with EFCL funds. It was later
proven that the trip was indeed authorized, although not by the whole board.

Another conflict, which began in October, involved a disciplinary investigation by the EFCL board of two fellow board members for "injuring the good

name of the organization." It was resolved when a defamation suit brought against Janice Fleming by the then executive director, Bernice Neufeld, was settled in 1997 out of court.

Amidst this highly emotional situation, the EFCL struggled to consolidate the operating grants that the city provided to each of the existing 142 community leagues. Because the size of the grants depended on the population of each league, amounts ranged from $3,355 to $3,955. The EFCL executive wanted to coordinate grant applications on behalf of the leagues to speed and simplify the process. It was a good idea; however, given the goings-on around the board, the leagues quickly rejected the notion and moved on with their first priority—to return the EFCL to a functional state.

According to EFCL records, the presidents of Area Councils 1 and 2, Jim Acton and Bill Maxim, the EFCL suffered from numerous problems including poor bookkeeping practices, deficit budgets, poor labour practices, and various controversies about the use of federation funds for unauthorized purposes. Their conclusion was that the city must conduct a forensic audit of EFCL finances for the previous five years. City council took the suggestion seriously, and in early December 1997, it held public hearings into the matter with speakers and councillors representing both sides of the debate.

Councillor Brent Maitson, a former president of the Riverbend Community League president and of the Southwest Area Council, argued for an audit. Councillor Allan Bolstad, a former Sherbrook Community League president, considered the situation serious enough to be addressed. Councillor Michael Phair argued that city council should avoid getting involved. Even the auditor general, Andre Bolduc, entered the debate, suggesting that a forensic audit was often a prelude to suspected criminal charges and should therefore be used sparingly and cautiously.

In the end, city council took a wait-and-see stance and agreed to give the federation an opportunity to sort out its affairs. The weight of the solution rested squarely on the shoulders of an EFCL task force that included three former federation presidents and two city appointees.

On November 24, 1997, the EFCL held its general meeting—an extremely significant event—at the Belmead Community League. According to the November 28 issue of the Edmonton Examiner, more than one hundred people packed the community hall, generally disregarding the agenda and debating for hours on the direction that their federation should take to "revitalize" itself. Eventually, the members committed to establishing a task force that would go ahead with its review—even if it received no support from city council—through the involvement of two council-appointed personnel. The fact that it took over two hours to reach that point reflected the internal bickering within the federation and caused much frustration to those attending. Don Kuchelyma, the EFCL vice-president of internal affairs, said, "We've got 143 members, 143 different opinions. Each one is right to a different degree." The difficilty in reaching a consensus is the problem, he added.

A few days later, according to the December 2 issue of the *Edmonton Journal*, city council decided to defer making a decision on a city-conducted forensic audit of the EFCL to the beginning of 1998. The move came in the hope that the EFCL could (and would) begin to sort itself out. However, on January 2, the *Edmonton Examiner* reported that most of council was ready to endorse a motion by Bolstad to audit the EFCL's financial records from 1992 to 1997. Bolstad stated, "The community league movement is too valuable to the city to allow it to whither and die. We have to step in and sort this out."

The same *Examiner* article reported that councillor Leroy Chahley said, "The problems in the EFCL stem from the people running it. 'If the same people stay, no matter what the auditor finds, says or recommends, nothing will change'." Five days later, the January 5 *Edmonton Journal* reported that council had debated the issue for over two hours before deciding to let the EFCL resolve its own problems. The article stated that EFCL president Wil Moore had requested a forensic audit of the EFCL by the city, but was "somewhat disappointed" that city council had refused his request. Moore, a former chair of the Southeast Communities Planning Coalition, recommended that the city distribute its annual administrative grant to the EFCL among the existing leagues. (The January 9 *Edmonton Examiner* reported a claim by Jim Acton that council had failed to support the forensic audit because of a looming municipal election, and councillors "didn't want to rock the boat.")

Meanwhile, infighting continued to plague the EFCL board, leaving it mired in accusations of mismanagement and manipulation. Much criticism resulted from the manner in which Moore was elected following Meyers's sudden resignation (for medical reasons). On March 13, the *Edmonton Examiner* reported the resignation of three board members—Sandy Guilbert, Elna Nash, and Jack Eldridge. Nash, who had served ten years on the board, complained, "I can't work with a president who is manipulating rules without facilitating open discussion on all issues." Nash also complained about the manipulation of Moore's election, which excluded the consideration of any other potential candidates.

This dysfunctional environment of sniping and acrimonious feuding gave birth to the Revitalization Task Force, which proved to be a blessing for the community league movement. At the EFCL's annual general meeting in late March 1998, those present worked hard to ensure the success of the Revitalization Task Force. Milestones and mechanisms established to guide the task force included a number of special meetings and information sessions, which were to prove extremely valuable in garnering the support of those who had hitherto been silent about their concerns.

To kick-start its revitalization effort[5], the EFCL hired an outside consultant and an EFCL past president, Leonard Apedaile, who surveyed numerous league representatives on the issues. The first draft of his report, *Grassroots Community Leaders Speak Out*, was presented in May with the final draft following in October. The report reflected 902 completed questionnaires returned from 117 of the existing 143 leagues, and all parts of the city. Its executive summary noted:

> Significant issues around the function and practice of the EFCL are raised by the survey. Respondents do not have adequate trust in the EFCL and are concerned about its competence to represent their leagues and to manage money. Communication practices are noted as ineffective and somewhat male oriented. The Board is too large. Geographic representation using the area council concept is problematic. Leaders are absolutely intolerant of conflict of interest on the Board between EFCL interests and political aspirations and agendas, whether real or perceived. Respondents demonstrate discomfort with the relationship between their leagues and agencies in the City of Edmonton. They view the most important service of the EFCL as to provide a supportive skilled companion for individual leagues as they pursue their interests with the City. (p. 2)

This report provided a good basis for the Revitalization Task Force, which included three EFCL past presidents—Arlene Meldrum, John Bracegirdle, and Don Eastcott—plus two people appointed by the City of Edmonton—Dick Haldane and Fred Tyrrell. The extensive credentials of the team members, added to their incredible passion and commitment to the community league movement, created an ideal task force. Meldrum brought over forty years of extensive service within community organizations in various roles including leadership, management, and training. Bracegirdle was a community liaison officer with the Community Facility Enhancement program of the Alberta Liquor and Gaming Commission. He was also actively involved within his southeast Edmonton community league and the Mill Woods Presidents' Council. Eastcott was a strategic planner, a businessperson, and a self-declared "social/economic philosopher." Haldane was a practising lawyer for twenty-five years, a past league president, and a former chair of the city's Parks, Recreation, and Cultural Advisory Board. Tyrrell was a community development officer with Alberta Community Development and a former recreation director with more than twenty-five years of community involvement.

The task force had a broad and tremendously challenging mandate, which it received from the EFCL membership at its annual general meeting on November 24, 1997. Essentially, it had to diagnose the EFCL as an organization and recommend remedial action for its return to functionality. More specifically, the task force was to review the EFCL purpose, bylaws, policies, structure, organization, and operational practices, as well as to ensure consultation with key stakeholders internal to the EFCL (the leagues and area councils) and external agencies like the city's departments.

The process was demanding and laborious, generating a small mountain of data through numerous interviews, meetings, and written submissions. Right from the start, issues met with consensus. Leading among them were the belief and expectations that:

1. Community leagues are valuable organizations in the City of Edmonton.
2. A valuable role is to be played by an umbrella organization, such as the E.F.C.L.

3. Community leagues are the owners of the federation. Community leagues must act to ensure that the E.F.C.L. is responsive to their needs and accountable to the community leagues. (EFCL Revitalization Task Force, p. 6)

On June 18, 1998, the task force presented its preliminary report to the EFCL membership. The document highlighted the value and positive impact that the community league movement had had on the quality of life in Edmonton. It reported that, in 1998, over 1,700 volunteers served on community league boards, another 120 on the area councils, and more than 30,000 residents volunteered for their local community league programs and services. In 1996, the leagues managed a total of $64,586,000 in assets, which included 126 community halls, 135 league-operated rinks, and 280 playgrounds. During the operational year 1995–96, the EFCL and its leagues spent nearly $15 million to operate their programs.

In 1998, every major neighbourhood across Edmonton had a league to represent its needs. (In 2002, the downtown core, long represented by the Rossdale Community League, became its own league—the Downtown Edmonton Community Association or DECA.) These leagues were busy serving over 228,000 of Edmonton's residents, and the demand for league services was increasing. For example, the leagues reported a 314-percent increase in the use of ice arenas and rinks since 1996. Collectively, the leagues provided their members with 718 winter hours and 200 summer hours of free public skating, as well as 1,098 hours of free public swimming at the city's pools. League halls were in demand and were being booked from eighteen to twenty-four months ahead of time. League-delivered recreational programs included soccer, hockey, ringette, softball, baseball, skating, lacrosse, basketball, and (at a few) tennis.

The interim report noted that the EFCL Talent Show involved over 1,000 youth, the Boysdale Camp hosted 400 disadvantaged youth, nearly 10,700 volunteers participated in the EFCL Neighbourhood Watch program, and countless league volunteers inventoried and monitored over 22,200 elm trees for the dreaded Dutch elm disease. The EFCL and its leagues were frequently interacting with eight separate city departments, and they provided benefits in five distinct areas: personal, social, environmental, infrastructure, and economic. The task force report also indicated that, besides its 142

Ridgewood Community League volunteers constructing a playground. EFCL collection.

community leagues, the EFCL also included eleven area councils and forty-two separate committees. Administered by the EFCL board, these organizations relied on four full-time staff and two summer students for support. The staff also produced a newsletter, distributed to the membership and external stakeholders ten times a year.

The task force identified three key issues, each with a myriad of related difficulties or obstacles needing remedy. These provided a clear perspective of the current operational environment as well as the depth of difficulty in which the community league movement found itself. The three issues, and their related obstacles, were outlined in its preliminary report:

1. The EFCL structure and organization reduce its ability to achieve its goals
   - Size of the board
   - Terms of office were too long
   - Composition of the board, which included voting members who were elected by and responsible to the Area Councils

In 1977, the EFCL's annual budget, not including sports or programs, was around $200,000. Based on volunteer time and output, the community league movement's contribution to the city that year was an estimated $32,988,820.

- Orientation and training of board members
- Practices affecting the management of board business were not grounded because of the lack of established, communicated, and adhered-to procedures
- Committee structure was hard to manage or coordinate
- Systems for planning, monitoring, evaluating, and redirecting of activities were lacking
- EFCL Bylaws were unclear and ambiguous
- Conflicting perspectives between groups (i.e., Area Councils) within the federation. The structure, mandate, and orientation of Area Council was not consistent, or always in support of the community league movement

2. Relationships with the City of Edmonton affect the role of community leagues and the federation
   - Citizen participation in the planning process, or the lack of consistency among members of the community league movement about the degree and scope of their participation regarding issues from recreation and sports to infrastructure and city services
   - Community infrastructure of programs and facilities, or the concern that increasingly leagues are expected by the city to pick up the slack and to do so with less and less public funds
   - Collaborative effort to support community leagues, especially between the city's Community Recreation Consultants (CRCs) and the EFCL

3. The EFCL and community leagues do not have a strong tradition or system for long-term planning.

On June 12, the *Edmonton Examiner* noted, "The report says factions do exist and have caused 'irreparable damage'. The report details geographic splits, personal agendas, positioning on issues perceived to be related to political aspirations, and a north-south split. North-side communities are more involved with facilities and programs, while the Southside tends to be more involved in community planning and social issues."

A day later, an *Edmonton Journal* city column lambasted the federation under the headline "Task Force Blasts Group, Wants It To Find Own Solutions." The article that followed outlined the highlights of the task force report and chastised the report's authors for leaving the EFCL and its membership without clear solutions to the identified problems. While the observation was accurate, the criticism was not! The task force's first priority was to identify the problems within the federation and report these to the membership—before reaching for its conclusions and recommendations.

The *Journal* exposed another perspective by reporting that, "perhaps the biggest problem facing the federation and community leagues is government downloading. The report points out that the city expects community leagues to raise thousands of dollars for playground replacement." Not only did leagues wishing to have a playground first have to raise the funds necessary to develop it, they then had to plan and work to meet increasingly restrictive city standards required for playground construction. League volunteers typically constructed the playground under the watchful eye of representatives from the city Community Services Department, who monitored the process to ensure adherence to standards. The leagues then turned the completed playgrounds over to the city's Community Services Department, which added the facility to Edmonton's list of assets. However, when playgrounds were in need of repair or upgrade—sometimes because of revised standards—the city again expected the leagues to raise the necessary funds and perform the repairs.

By October 1998, when the task force completed its final report, the EFCL had a clear direction toward its yet-to-be-finalized destination. "We are firm believers that the EFCL has to be accountable to its members," said task force member Dick Haldane in the October 9 *Edmonton Examiner*, which reported that the task force had recommended six clear actions:

- the mandate of the EFCL had to be defined, and was best done by the leagues
- the Leagues needed to develop a suitable system of governance that would work for their federation
- the EFCL and the City needed to define the relationship between the city, the federation and its leagues
- the EFCL needed to develop a comprehensive communication system
- the leagues needed to amend the EFCL Bylaws, to provide for the election of a three-person "interim management committee" to maintain all essential services while the federation was undergoing its revitalization process
- a five-member revitalization implementation team was to be elected to lead and coordinate the revitalization process

Only three days earlier, the *Edmonton Journal* had given its own take on the report, advised of the upcoming November 23 meeting at which the report would be debated, and warned about the mood within the federation. It quoted Cindy Nolan, the Forest Heights Community League president whose league is one of the federation's founding members, as saying, "There are so many of who have given up [on the federation]. They're tired of the bickering. They're tired of the politics. They need to come to that meeting and take (the federation) back …. They can get in here and save it, or they [can] kiss it goodbye."

The mood, shared by many league representatives, reflected the frustration they felt with what they considered were a few bad apples. Wil Moore—the federation president who had pushed unsuccessfully for a forensic audit of the EFCL by the city was also quoted in the article, saying, "Too much has been made of what's wrong with the federation." He added that he felt optimistic that the process begun that Monday could work.

The October 9 issue of the *Edmonton Examiner* also quoted a number of league representatives who were concerned with what they perceived as the slow pace of the revitalization process and with the involvement of those perceived by the membership to be part of the problem.

"I challenge all members of the board to abstain from voting," said board member Elna Nash. Parkallen league representative and lawyer Michael Pucylo agreed, and added that board members should not vote on task force recommendations due to potential conflict of interest. South Clareview league representative Johanna Tardiff emphasized her need to get approval for the EFCL's new direction from her league and suggested holding special league meetings to move the process forward expeditiously. A clear message was sent by many league representatives that it was "now or never" for the federation.

The EFCL general meeting of November 23, 1998, held at the Westmount community hall, was a milestone for the EFCL. An emotional meeting seemed to pit a number of EFCL board members against frustrated and angry community league representatives. A key point of contention was whether board members were to vote on the task force recommendations and the bylaws revision. Moore, the meeting chair, deemed a motion to remove the voting rights of the board members out of order, but Ritchie league representative Hardy Schafer immediately challenged the ruling. Parkallen's Pucylo said that "there is a potential for conflict of interest if board members do vote tonight." John Logan, vice-president of the Bonnie Doon Community League, agreed and noted, "It appears to me as a lay person it would be in violation of fundamental principles of fairness if the board was to vote on its own fate." In the end, Schafer's challenge succeeded. All EFCL board members were excluded from voting on the future of the EFCL—a drastic but necessary stand, one that helped to restore the EFCL ownership to its league members.

The meeting was pivotal in that it resulted in the approval (77% voted in favour) of new EFCL bylaws, which immediately reduced the EFCL board from its inflated size of 43 to 3 members! However, the presence of only one candidate for the job, Charlie Galan, created a problem with continuity of governance. There was concern, that by accepting the bylaws without the presence of a new board, the EFCL would cripple itself. The solution, again arrived at after much wrangling, was to recess the meeting until January 18, 1999, by which time it was hoped that other candidates would step forward. This gave the federation some time, but left many of its members wondering about the future of their organization.

At the end of the meeting, six board members handed in their resignation, partly because of their exclusion from the new EFCL board. The federation membership, frustrated by the infighting within the EFCL board, passed a resolution excluding all individuals who had been involved with the board during the last five years from participating on the new board. It was another drastic step, one that excluded many good-intentioned, hard-working,

The pool at the Boysdale camp.
EFCL collection.

and dedicated volunteers. However, it reflected the leagues' frustration with EFCL management and their determination to regain control over their federation.

As if the struggle to revitalize was not enough of a challenge, the EFCL was busy with another issue—the Boysdale Camp. Over the years, Boysdale had provided thousands of disadvantaged children from Edmonton with the opportunity to go to camp, and that aspect was encouraged and supported by the leagues. However, their dissatisfaction with the camp's management festered and required increasing attention. The difficulties, visible decades earlier, involved the relationship between the federation and the governance of the camp.

In 1965, EFCL President George Hughes had removed the camp's board of trustees (under Steve Wyker) and replaced them with a new board involving league representatives. At issue was the board's lack of accountability to the EFCL, and unauthorized expenditures. Two years later, in order to access funds from the United Community Fund (renamed the United Way in 1973), the camp had applied for and received (as a committee of the EFCL) charitable status from Revenue Canada. By 1976, the EFCL treasurer had become a member of the camp's board, which received access to the EFCL bingo as a fund-generating opportunity.

Then, in 1979, in an effort to enhance the camp board's fundraising ability, the EFCL allowed it to incorporate as a Part 9 company in the Alberta Corporate Registry. (This form of incorporation was more flexible than the traditional incorporation as a society.) The EFCL motion authorized the move with the understanding that the new entity would be "a wholly owned subsidiary of the EFCL." One hundred shares were issued by the newly created Boysdale Camp Foundation, ninety-nine held by the EFCL through its president and one in trust by its lawyer. The creation of the Boysdale Camp Foundation as a Part 9 company proved to be a colossal mistake.

On May 22, 1980, a fire in the camp, allegedly due to a malfunction with the hot water heater in the old kitchen, resulted in the loss of some records about the camp and its management. A year later the United Way ruled that the Boysdale Camp Foundation had violated its campaign conditions, resulting in the loss of its campaign licence, which eliminated a major opportunity to access available funds. In 1990, the lawyer for the EFCL (and the Boysdale Camp Foundation) warned that the camp's annual income tax return was well overdue and there was a risk that its charitable status might be lost—which it was. In an effort to resolve the problem, the EFCL transferred the title to the camp's land to the Boysdale Camp Foundation board in the hope that the transfer would convince Revenue Canada that the EFCL could not gain access to Boysdale property upon the camp's dissolution. The transfer of land was a monumental debacle for the EFCL, and would return to haunt the 1999 board of directors.

By 1992, the Boysdale Camp Foundation board discovered that its treasurer, a family member of a Boysdale board member, had absconded with $78,538.68 of foundation funds. An additional $15,000 went missing the following year. Negotiations to recover the money, conducted secretly, remained out of the media and away from the membership. In 1993, the Boysdale Camp Foundation treasurer paid $13,000 as restitution. The relative, who was also a board member, signed a release deeming all debts collected.

Predictably, tension continued to mount between the EFCL and the Boysdale Camp Foundation board, although the former continued to support camp operations. In 1994, the EFCL helped Boysdale with storage of its files and development of a five-year plan. It also included the Boysdale Camp Foundation in its blanket insurance policy.

> The Boysdale Camp summertime operation lasted from its inception in 1948 until 2002. It closed in 2003, reportedly due to maintenance problems, but re-opened in 2004. During its many years of operation, Boysdale Camp provided a tremendous opportunity for thousands of underprivileged children, who were sent to the camp for a week at a time.

By the end of 1998, the relationship between the EFCL and the Boysdale Camp Foundation had deteriorated to a point of mistrust. It seemed that the same names and issues were repeatedly popping up on the Boysdale board and frequently appearing on the EFCL agenda, often with a request for more funds or volunteer support from the leagues. The leagues (and the EFCL) were increasingly tired of supporting the camp without the accountability that they expected of their own organization—the EFCL board. The Boysdale Camp Foundation's relationship with the Boys and Girls Club had also deteriorated significantly. A year earlier, when the Boysdale board had refused to sign a memorandum of understanding regarding respective roles and responsibilities at the camp, the Boys and Girls Club walked away. This, too, was significant, especially given the long-term involvement and contribution of the Boys and Girls Club to camp operations during the summer months by supplying councillors and other qualified personnel.

Then, there were the community leagues that continued to serve as the main thread of the movement, and gave it stability, and a solid foundation. Throughout this period of turmoil, the leagues continued to work diligently to deliver countless of programs. Recreation, sports, the local infrastructure, and quality of life issues continued to dominate the agenda at local level. Seeing or hearing of the turmoil within the EFCL board, some chose to stay away and do their own thing. Nevertheless, many did jump into the fray to move the federation away from the brink and into a revitalized mode.

Many issues dealt with through the leagues were resolved successfully, but a few were not. Among the latter group was the construction of a McDonald's fast-food outlet at 109th Street and 61st Avenue. Residents of Parkallen, Pleasant View, and Allendale protested that development on grounds that it attracted

Meal time at the Boysdale camp.
EFCL collection.

youth to a dangerously busy traffic intersection. Despite much effort by the leagues and their supporters on council, the battle was lost and the outlet was established. Nevertheless, the leagues gained from the affair, since it raised the standard of the municipal planning requirement for community consultation. The notification standard, revisited a few years later, brought about greater awareness by the city planning department regarding the need to involve the community league movement early in the planning or development process.

On that note, the March 13, 1998, issue of the *Edmonton Examiner* reported the development of an EFCL committee to review proposed standards for parkland development, sports fields, schools, and community league facilities. The committee, chaired by Bryce Card, was also tasked with reviewing the standards for the booking, use, and fee structure for sports fields and gymnasiums.

The 1990s were indeed a tough period for the leagues and their federation. The EFCL was heavily involved in consultations with the city over its planning process. This started with Mayor Reimer and the Mayor's Task Force on the Planning Process and continued through to the recent transportation master plan and the rewrite of the land use bylaw. Significant effort went into these projects. This period also involved tremendous upheavals that again saw the leagues become more politically involved.

For example, in April 1994, more than 15,000 protesters marched to the Grey Nuns Hospital in Mill Woods in objection to the Klein government's intended cuts to this state-of-the-art facility, completed less than a decade earlier. This was the largest demonstration in Edmonton to date, bar none. (Another march at the same location took place on September 9 and involved an estimated 25,000 people.) In the end, the protesters won their battle and the province left "their hospital" almost untouched.

Similarly, the leagues won their internally fought battle to retain control of their organization. By the end of 1998, the leagues had established a new direction for the revitalized federation, set new bylaws for it, and nervously waited for the opportunity to elect their new board. Their next meeting, slated for January 18, 1999, was to be critical. Indeed it was, and it started the federation on its way again.

Alone we can do so little;
together we can do so much.
— HELEN KELLER

7

Reinventing
and Reinvesting

1999–2004

Coming together is a beginning;
Keeping together is a process;
Working together is success.

— HENRY FORD

THE LAST FEW YEARS LEADING TO THE NEW MILLENNIUM saw high activity in many sectors. The dreaded Y2K bug—the Year 2000 computer glitch predicted to threaten the continued operations of many computer chips beyond January 1, 2000—triggered a significant part of the activity. Many companies across Edmonton and Alberta seemed vulnerable, especially in the utilities, petrochemical, travel, and banking sectors. Local preparations reflected a challenging and costly effort, totalling in the billions of dollars, across the globe. However, after all the hype, the new millennium rolled in almost uneventfully. Fortunately, the tremendous cost and effort was not wasted. It left two important legacies: the exposure of serious operational vulnerabilities, and the encouragement (perhaps forced) toward upgrading of computer chip-dependent equipment.

Fortunately for Alberta and Edmonton, too, their economies during the late 1990s and early 2000s were strong and growing steadily. In part, this strength reflected massive investments in Fort McMurray's oil sands development and oil refinery fields, and the newly opened diamond mines in the north. As the *Edmonton Journal* noted, "Edmonton is the major service and supply centre for a

Edmonton's Folk Festival celebrations, circa 2003.
Courtesy Edmonton Tourism/Edmonton Economic Development Corporation.

$60-billion wave of economic activity sweeping across Northern Alberta—the largest concentration of economic activity anywhere in the world." For the first time since 1980, overall construction in Edmonton surpassed the $1-billion mark. The growth of single residential homes also mushroomed, with 4,412 building permits issued in 2002, breaking the previous record set in 1979.

Quite predictably, Edmonton's population continued to grow. Housing development along the city's boundaries proceeded rapidly, especially in the northeast, southeast, southwest, and west. New residents flocked to Edmonton and Alberta, lured by the burgeoning economy. The greater number of ethnic restaurants, stores, and structures such as temples and ethnic community halls reflected the increasing diversity of the city's population. On December 11, 1999, the first Mormon temple opened in Edmonton. This was only the province's second temple since the construction of the Cardston temple in southern Alberta in 1923.

The growing population placed increasing demands on the local and provincial infrastructure, including health, education, transportation, housing, and even the phone system. On January 25, 1999, Edmonton and northern

Alberta were switched to a new area code (780), with the rest of the province retaining the 403 area code. It was a direct indication of the population growth across the province, as well as the popularity and increasing proliferation of technology. More telephones, faxes, computer-dedicated lines, and cellular phones created a proliferation of numbers that could not be sustained by a single area code.

Edmonton's downtown core, a major concern during the previous two decades, underwent a transformation. Modern loft apartments and office buildings replaced previously neglected buildings, while other buildings, like the City Centre complex, received costly but worthwhile renovations. These developments encouraged retail businesses to relocate nearby, giving the area a more inviting "new" look.

The late twentieth century was also a period of continued infrastructure growth and upgrading, especially relating to transportation routes. The 109th Street "Rat Hole," an underpass built in 1927, had served the city well, but in later years it became an impediment to the increasingly heavier traffic. Severe downpours also affected it, such as during the 1987 tornado when the Rat Hole flooded. Its demolition was part of a larger revitalization project in the downtown area, which saw the removal of the old railway lines and their replacement with the main campus of the Grant MacEwan Community College, shops, and condominiums.

There were also a number of major highway construction projects. One such project involving the Anthony Henday Highway continued along Edmonton's western flank as part of a ring road bypass route around the city. A project in Edmonton's eastern edge, scheduled for completion in late 2004 or early 2005, involved a long-overdue overpass on Whitemud Drive at 34th Street. A safer and more efficient interchange on Gateway Boulevard (formerly the Calgary Trail) at 23rd Avenue, in the city's south end, is due for completion by 2010.

During 2002, city council broke with its long-term fiscal tradition and agreed to go into debt to finance major projects across the city, voting to borrow up to $250 million in $50-million annual increments to augment its budget. It borrowed the first $50 million for the 2003 budget. A year later, it again went into debt and allocated another $50 million for projects identified in the 2004 budget. This commitment spurred development and expectations at all levels.

Much of the earlier borrowing went to roadway upgrades and the establishment of a district-level police station in Mill Woods. The second instalment went to highway development. The city was putting its money where its mouth was. After all, it was the "City of Champions!" (The 2002 public debate about the city's motto, which raised a wide range of possible alternatives, ultimately resulted in it remaining "City of Champions.")

Edmonton's residents were rightly proud of their "champions" and continued to be interested in and supportive of sports and recreation, but with greater intensity. They continued to follow the fortunes of the Oilers and the "Great One"—Wayne Gretzky, who was inducted on November 22, 1999, into the Hockey Hall of Fame. (Around that time, the Capilano Freeway was renamed Wayne Gretzky Way.) On March 21, 2001, two of Edmonton's sweethearts, skaters Jamie Sale and David Pelletier, won a gold medal at the World Figure Skating Championships. The two lived in Edmonton and trained at the local rink of the Glenora Club, which was also the training ground for Kurt Browning and Kristi Yamaguchi. A few months later, during late July 2001, Edmonton again was host to an international sports event—the World Triathlon Championships. A month later, on August 3, Edmonton again served as host, this time to the World Athletics Championships.

On September 1, 2002, Edmonton hosted the Fédération Internationale de Football Association (FIFA) under-19 women's soccer world championship before a record crowd of 47,784 fans at Commonwealth Stadium. In football, the city hosted the Grey Cup in November 24, 2002, when the Eskimos battled the Montreal Alouettes only to lose 25 to 16. Basketball too received a boost. The January 21, 2004, *Edmonton Journal* reported that the city had identified land for the construction of "a $10-million, not-for-profit Edmonton Grads Basketball Centre." The centre, in memory of the city's incredible and internationally renowned basketball team of the 1920s and 1930s, would include space to house the Grads archives, nine courts, and seating sufficient for 3,500 spectators. The *Journal* also reported, "Impressively, only 38 players ever played in the Grads' colours. Ten of them are still alive."

Across Alberta, the general sense of prosperity was interspersed with calamities that slowed some of the economic momentum. A crippling drought across southern Alberta in 2002 resulted in massive shortages of feed for livestock. This was especially devastating for the large cattle industry and the

In 2004, Ron Hayter was re-elected to Edmonton's city council and started his twenty-eighth year on council. Hayter is Edmonton's longest-serving councillor, having won ten civic elections since 1971. In the presentation of his Queen's Golden Jubilee Medal, his success was ascribed to his "extraordinary commitment of time, energy and talent to the political and community life of his city, province and country."

A resident of Edmonton since 1960, Hayter has volunteered his services with countless organizations and ventures. These involved more than twenty-five civic boards and organizations including the Edmonton Police Commission, the Klondike Days Association, Canadian Native Friendship Centre, Edmonton Public Library Board, and the Old Strathcona Foundation. He is also a past president of the Alberta Urban Municipalities Association and the Federation of Canadian Municipalities.

Hayter has been a long-time promoter of sports and recreation. A founding member of the International Baseball Federation, he played a key role in getting baseball recognized as an Olympic sport. As a founding director of the 1978 Commonwealth Games, he played a pivotal role in attracting these games to Edmonton. He was also instrumental in attracting six international baseball events to Edmonton since 1980, including the first-ever World Cup of Women's Baseball in 2004.

A staunch supporter of the community league movement, Hayter has worked tirelessly to increase and improve amateur and professional sport facilities in Edmonton. His efforts led to civic recognition of the value of community league involvement in the planning, development, and enhancement of the city. He spearheaded the grant program for community leagues, the development of permanent office for the Edmonton Federation of Community Leagues (EFCL), and the civic requirement to notify leagues of proposed developments or planning changes in their area.

Hayter also staunchly supported the preservation of Edmonton's beautiful river valley. "The community leagues in Edmonton have never had a better friend than Ron Hayter," said

Bill Maxim in 1996 when presenting him an award on behalf of Area Council 2.

Hayter received the Vanier Award in 1974 as one of Canada's "Outstanding Young Canadians" and the Government of Alberta Achievement Award in 1975 for "excellence in community service." He was inducted into the Edmonton and Alberta Sports Halls of Fame and the Canadian Boxing Hall of Fame; he is also a lifetime member of the Federation of Canadian Municipalities, the Alberta Urban Municipalities Association, the TransCanada-Yellowhead Highway Association, the Western Canada Baseball Association, and Baseball Alberta. In January 2000, Hayter was selected by the *Edmonton Journal* as one of the top 100 Edmontonians of the twentieth century, as well as one of the city's "movers and shakers" in sports during the past one hundred years.

---

businesses that supported its operations. The results were felt across the province as farmers struggled to feed their livestock. In response to their plight, Ontario and Quebec farmers helped organize the "Hay West campaign"—a massive collection and transportation of feed to Western farms. The provincial and federal government eventually contributed to reduce (but not eliminate) the financial burden on the farming community.

Then, in spring 2003, Toronto became the centre of attention when it experienced an outbreak of the hitherto unknown Sudden Acute Respiratory Syndrome. SARS quickly became a household term that gave much concern to those who travelled through the international airport. Shortly thereafter, another term, BSE or mad cow disease, became a widespread topic, after a single cow infected by bovine spongiform encephalopathy triggered almost immediately the shutdown of cross-border transportation of beef between Canada and its trading partners, most notably the United States. Yet, amid these calamities, Edmonton's economy continued to grow and Edmonton's residents continued to revitalize their city.

On January 7, 2002, the Third Battalion of the Edmonton-based Princess Patricia's Canadian Light Infantry (PPCLI) regiment left for active duty in Afghanistan. It was an emotional farewell for Edmonton, and a monumental

Klondike Days celebration at the Midway.
Courtesy Edmonton Tourism/Edmonton Economic Development Corporation.

step for Canada. This was the first combat assignment for Canadian troops since the Korean War in the early 1950s, and an assignment that kept "our boys" in the public eye. Then came April 18, 2002, a day of great sadness for Edmonton. The *Edmonton Journal*'s headlines announced that on the previous day in a military training area on the other side of the world, in Afghanistan, an American F-16 jet had mistakenly bombed the PPCLI troops, killing four and injuring others.

Amid prosperity, many issues of old persisted: funding for health care, education, municipal infrastructure, recreation, and others. Often, the funding for these services seemed like a hot potato bounced from one level of government to another and back again, with little resolution and much frustration to the taxpayers.

The rush to upgrade, modernize, and revitalize also hit the EFCL, but for a different reason. The federation had to revitalize and complete the arduous task set for it by the Revitalization Task Force in 1998. The process was not easy, and it soon became more complicated by another festering problem—the Boysdale Camp Foundation.

The task force's recommendation to establish a much-reduced board was difficult to fulfill. One call for nominations, in late 1998, resulted in only a single volunteer who was prepared to put his neck in the proverbial organizational noose. At the EFCL's next general meeting, on January 18, 1999, the situation was not much better. There were three candidates for the sure-to-be challenging task of getting the federation back on track. The membership elected Charlie Galan, Eric Mahabir, and Ron Kuban by acclamation. It was the first time the three had met, but they soon blended their talents and assumed three critical roles: president (Kuban), vice-president (Galan), and treasurer (Mahabir). Galan, president of the Lynwood Community League, was a professional mediator in private practice. Mahabir, soccer coordinator for the Duggan league and president of the southwest zone of the Edmonton Minor Soccer Association, was an investigator with the provincial government. Kuban, president of the Meadows Community League, operated a consulting company specializing in crisis management. They were the right team for the time.

Soon afterward, the three-person board was augmented by the Revitalization Implementation Team, which was elected to build upon the task force's recommendations and translate them into an operational framework that included mandate, bylaws, guidelines, and organizational structure. The team included Bill Brown of Lorelei-Beaumaris, Donna Fong of Strathcona, Michael Pucylo of Parkallen, Don Weideman of Oliver, and Guntram Beringer of Parkview, who passed away early in the committee's term (September 1999).

The implementation team members had an onerous task, an often-skeptical audience, and short timelines. It would have been a losing proposition if not for the team's dogged determination and the support received from the EFCL executive director, Bernice Neufeld. Through many long meetings, often well past midnight, the team managed to cobble together a framework that withstood the membership's inspection.

The Revitalization Implementation Team organized a number of focus groups and other meetings to gather the views of league and stakeholder representatives, as well as feedback on certain proposals. Based on this data, the team framed the focus and existing challenges for the community league movement, beginning with the federation's mission statement: "to enhance the quality of life in Edmonton by supporting the community league movement." The task force's report also outlined the beliefs and values of the community league movement and its umbrella organization, the EFCL:

> Quality of Life—The EFCL has had a positive impact in terms of community development in Edmonton.
> Volunteerism—This is fundamental to and the most valuable resource of the community league movement. Volunteerism is a spirit, an attitude and an integral part of our culture.
> Volunteers—Must be provided with opportunities to develop skills ... with support and information provided by the EFCL.
> Security and Safety—Residents feel secure taking part in activities that are league supported and sanctioned. Children in the community have a safe place to play that is easily accessible and affordable.
> Healthy Sport and Recreation—Community-based recreation, leisure activities and life skills programs offer affordable, accessible activities for league members, providing the added benefit of healthier, happier community residents.
> Sense of Community and Belonging.
> Sense of Place—League halls and other community facilities provide meeting places for adults and children.
> Partnerships and Linkages.

The Revitalization Implementation Team presented its first formal report,[1] *Mandate and Structure Recommendations*, a preliminary discussion paper, at the EFCL's January 2000 general meeting. It identified a number of challenges:

- financial management of shrinking funds
- inadequate time to reflect upon or re-evaluate current situations
- lack of [sufficient number of] volunteers, burnout among existing volunteers, recruitment methods, and differences of opinion (i.e., egos and personal agendas of volunteers)

- knowing how best to communicate with a diversity of league representatives and in competition with a number of other information priorities
- volunteer time and money is siphoned off by competing organizations
- duplication of services by other non-profit organizations
- municipal downloading of recreation and leisure services and possibly social programs to community leagues, without adequate resource planning
- volunteers' knowledge of and compliance with ongoing changes in legislation or Bylaws
- recognition of league representatives' authority by other agencies

The implementation team defined the EFCL's services, which included: program delivery (e.g., social, recreational, sports), support of league volunteers (e.g., recruitment, recognition), provision of education or resources for boards and individuals, exchange of information, advocating on behalf of the leagues or the movement, and providing economy of scale (e.g., through bulk purchasing). The five identified objectives were:

- to facilitate healthy and safe communities by promoting participation in affordable recreation, sports and social activities at community level
- to promote, facilitate, and celebrate volunteerism at the community league level
- to develop and enhance the skills of community league volunteers by providing information, resources and education
- to provide a multi-dimensional communication network to share pertinent and timely information, including emerging trends
- to advocate on behalf of community leagues on general citywide issues and to assist member leagues in their roles as advocates

Key among the preliminary report's numerous recommendations was the suggestion to have the city divided into twelve districts, each including a number of community leagues that were to elect their own district representative. The new EFCL board consisted of the twelve district representatives only, each with a single vote. In this manner, all 144 leagues had a representative on the EFCL board of directors with equal vote—a significant change from the pre-revitalization period, when the board's power base depended on the geography of its members and their political alignment. Another significant change related to the length of time that board members could remain on the board.

The Federation of Calgary Communities (FCC), the EFCL's southern partner, and some of Edmonton's area councils provided the EFCL with valuable lessons. The former provided ways to avoid the pitfalls of the latter, where a few individuals had remained at the helm for decades. Based on the FCC model, the Revitalization Implementation Team decided that elections to the board would be restricted to two-year terms. Board members could be re-elected, but could serve no more than three terms in the same position, with a limit of six years of continuous service. Such an arrangement would allow for fresh ideas and regular rejuvenation, as well as restrict the ability of board members to assume "ownership" of the board or the federation.

After receiving general approval from the membership, the Revitalization Implementation Team turned its attention to its most critical task—completing the organizational framework and drafting bylaws. One of the initial challenges related to the boundaries of the districts, which needed to be balanced and structured fairly. They had to follow existing league boundaries so that no one league ended across two districts, and also to follow logical geographic boundaries such as the North Saskatchewan River or main transportation arteries. Each district had to respect diverse league-related culture or history, as well as existing working relationships among leagues. At the end, the implementation team presented the membership with a couple of scenarios for consideration.

In March 2000, at the EFCL annual general meeting, the implementation team presented its final report, titled *Foundation for the Future*, which clearly laid out a set of recommendations covering the federation's role in scholarships, committee structure and operations, election, district boundaries, code of ethics (see Appendix 3), the roles of each board position, and a set of bylaws. The membership accepted the report.

Meanwhile, the EFCL board was madly trying to stem the flood of issues that were swamping its three members. Each board member had his own task: Mahabir, to restore credibility to EFCL's accounting and financial processes; Galan (ever the mediator), to smooth relations with as many internal stakeholders as possible; and Kuban, to mend external fences and restore faith in the

EFCL President Ron Kuban and logo designer Joan Heys Hawkins
unveiling the new EFCL logo, October 2001.
EFCL collection.

federation as an operational entity. From the start, the three board members
stood united in their belief that the existence of the revitalized EFCL depended
upon open communication, fair dealing, and clear accountability. The board
was equally convinced that the existing 144 community leagues were the rightful
"owners" of the federation and had every right to know what the EFCL was (or
was not) doing on their behalf.

The conviction of the three board members quickly translated into
profound changes in how the federation conducted its business. Minutes of board
and general membership meetings were made readily available, initially in hard
copy but soon via the EFCL's website (www.efcl.org). Another major change
tackled the long established practice of taping all board meetings and general
meetings, with the recordings available to verify the contents of the minutes.

The "he-said, she-said" mistrust over these tapes reflected the animosity
and infighting that had permeated federation business. After a little over a year,
the membership developed enough trust in the revised federation's way of doing
business to agree to terminate the practice of taping meetings. The federation
newsletter was then used to communicate directly with community league

representatives. However, one obstacle persisted—league representatives did not always continue the communication flow to their league (i.e., its executive board or residents). That problem was somewhat reduced by the evolution of the EFCL website to include key parts of the newsletter.

Re-establishing faith in the federation as an entity was a major task for the board and executive director Neufeld, who had extensive knowledge and experience within the community league movement. The task was as demanding internally with the leagues as it was externally with the EFCL partners, which included city council and members of the Community Services Department. The relationship with city council became stronger through a number of face-to-face meetings and countless updates. City council also wanted some advice on balancing recognition of the EFCL and the community league movement with the growing power of some of the area councils. The federation consistently reminded council members that they had enshrined the authority of the EFCL and the community leagues as representatives of their community.

At an informal fact-finding meeting held in early 1999 between the new EFCL board and the area council presidents—all members of the previous EFCL board—the latter clearly stated that they would not support the federation in its revitalization or its new direction. Some were emphatic in their belief that the EFCL had outlived its usefulness and that their area council needed to become the voice of the area (and its community leagues). That meeting led nowhere, and thereafter the relationship between the EFCL and the area councils remained cordial but cool. The next contact would not occur until late 2003.

Overall, the process of reinvigorating the EFCL was working, albeit painfully slowly for the board and the Revitalization Implementation Team. Nevertheless, each contact brought it further away from the brink and to an increasing level of credibility and accountability. Now the Boysdale Camp Foundation needed attention.

When the new EFCL board assumed its duties in January 1999, it was quickly swamped with issues. At the time, the Boysdale Camp Foundation did not seem to be one of them, and the board assumed that all was well in that area. By late May, the Boysdale board was gearing up for another summer of camp operations. However, by then signs of underlying problems had begun to surface.

The first occurred when two Boysdale Camp Foundation board members approached Galan and Kuban to assist in a dispute involving another Boysdale board member. They were advised to follow up on the matter within the framework of their own board and ensure that action was taken to reduce potential liability for the camp and its board. The EFCL board offered its services as the next formal step in the process. A similar message went, shortly thereafter, to the Boysdale president, Reg Norby, who confirmed within the following two months that he had addressed the matter with the individual. By early July, other concerns about the Boysdale Foundation's management of the camp arose, and steadily the issue crept onto the EFCL board's agenda as it insisted on greater accountability and openness by the Boysdale Camp Foundation—as was expected of the EFCL in its revitalization process.

The relationship between the two boards grew tenser and on October 12, 1999, Kuban called a joint meeting. He voiced the EFCL's concern with the management practices of the Boysdale board; Norby and the Boysdale board insisted that they were independent and not accountable to the EFCL. The meeting was unproductive. Complying with existing bylaws, and representing the majority (99%) shareholder in BCF, Kuban then gave notice to the BCF board of a BCF shareholders' general meeting scheduled for December 6th.

It never materialized. Instead, on October 12 members of Boysdale board arrived at the EFCL offices and removed their new computer equipment and other resources and files. Then, on November 23, the day of an EFCL general meeting, the Boysdale board advised the EFCL that it no longer held controlling shares in the Boysdale Camp Foundation.

As a Class 9 Corporation, the Boysdale Camp Foundation board could, and did, issue itself new shares. In a letter dated November 23, Norby advised the EFCL that the Boysdale board had met the previous day and "unanimously resolved that membership in the Foundation must be expanded to reflect its community involvement and spirit. Therefore, a total of 420 shares in the authorized capital of Boysdale Camp Foundation were issued" to members of an augmented board. (Participation in this pivotal meeting excluded the two EFCL representatives and shareholders.) The Boysdale board members issued themselves 35 shares each at a value of $1 and diluted the EFCL control from 99 percent to a mere 19.5 percent. (The one-dollar value per share does not seem to reflect the nearly $2-million value of the Boysdale Camp land and its facilities, including an in-ground pool.) The board also declared that no Boysdale Camp Foundation shares could be sold or donated without the agreement of the board.

The EFCL board perceived the manoeuvre as unethical. When the EFCL membership learned of the matter at its regular meeting that evening, it reacted strongly with disbelief and anger, moving "that the EFCL board be given the authority to ascertain the position and take steps necessary to protect the EFCL's interest." Accordingly, in January 2000, the EFCL board filed a statement of claim against the Boysdale Camp Foundation specifically naming each of its board members. A long battle began over what many of the community leagues perceived as their rightful possession and to correct what they believed was an obvious ethical wrong.

At the federation's next general meeting, on February 9, the EFCL membership committed a significant amount of money to its legal battle with the Boysdale Camp Foundation and passed a motion "that legal action against BCF must continue by the board and any subsequent board until this issue is resolved, unless mediation or agreement is made." From then on, the "BCF issue" drained an inordinate amount of the EFCL board's attention and energy. Countless attempts to facilitate negotiation or mediation ended in failure. Some came close, but the Boysdale board typically rejected agreements between the respective lawyers.

As of early 2005, the matter remained unresolved. That is most unfortunate because it inaccurately casts a shadow on the Boysdale Camp itself. At its September 2000 meeting, the EFCL membership passed a resolution supporting a number of key principles that included:

EFCL supports the charitable purpose and activities of the Boysdale Camp in providing a summer camping experience for disadvantaged youth in Edmonton. It is the EFCL intent that the Boysdale Camp continues to survive and prosper.

Boysdale Camp has historically provided a significant benefit to the communities and leagues of Edmonton and ought to continue to do so.

The interest of Boysdale Camp would best be served if groups such as community leagues and stakeholder groups held the ownership of the camp.

While extremely demanding on limited time and resources, the Boysdale Camp Foundation issue did not preclude other EFCL activities, such as the provincial government's review of its gaming regulations governing primarily

The EFCL booth at Vitalize conference for volunteers, 2001. Left to right, back row: Glen Ampelford, Curtis Vornbrock. Front row: Bernice Neufeld (Executive Director), Loretta Richter, Joan Heys Hawkins, Kim Barclay, Linda Crosby, Edna McGeough. EFCL collection.

bingos and casinos, which were being reviewed with the intent of tightening eligibility for access and the rules on such things as the awarding of "credits" or "vouchers" for those who worked them. This was a big issue for the community leagues, which depended extensively on revenues from both bingos and casinos. Elimination of the credit vouchers that leagues were allowed to provide to their workers for use toward league-related programs would hurt their fundraising ability. The vouchers allowed financially disadvantaged parents to offset some of the cost of their children's involvement in league sports and recreational activities. After receiving input from the federation and countless community leagues, the review resulted in tighter regulations on accountability of gaming practices and funds, with the voucher system being retained.

Another massive effort by the EFCL related to the intended development by Edmonton's utility company—EPCOR—at its Rossdale site. The utility company wanted to remove a portion of the existing power plant and replace it with a more modern facility. This was met by two major objections: one, that the site was a rare (for Canada) historical site (a First Nations burial ground and a site of the early incarnation of Fort Edmonton) and two, that the intended development would further degrade the river valley. The Alberta Energy and Utilities Board held a six-week-long hearing, with lengthy presentations made by the federation in partnership with the Central Area Council of Community Leagues, Rossdale Community League, and First Nations groups. In a subsequent hearing at the Historical Resources Conservation Board, their arguments won the day and the intended demolition of the facility halted—though the future of the site remains uncertain.

In a similar vein, the federation went to bat on behalf of a number of leagues in the northwest part of the city, near the Inland Cement plant. This well-established plant had depended for many years on the use of gas-burning technology to facilitate its cement production. When increased gas prices led the company to apply to burn coal instead, the threat of the residue chemicals and carcinogens from coal burning got the neighbourhood residents fired up, especially considering the number of failures the company had had with its emission control devices. The residents organized themselves and secured, at an EFCL general meeting, the federation's assistance. Again, the federation stood by its community leagues and argued to stop the conversion. After much effort, the outcome was in favour of the leagues.

Another long-term struggle involved increasing vandalism to league facilities—community halls, ice rinks, playgrounds—and its effects on area residents. One notable example, reported in a September 4, 1999, article of the Edmonton Journal, involved the torching of the Kenilworth community hall on July 4, 1998, by vandals playing with its gas line. The community league's vice-president and a member of the building committee reflected that vandals "have no idea of the cost of [their vandalism] and the emotional upset of it. It's really heartbreaking after putting in all this time and effort and money. It's hard not to take it personally, because it's almost like our home." This was the third torching of a community hall in six years—the Elmwood Park community hall had burned in May 1993 and the Central McDougall community hall in August 1995—and it served as a major warning for all the leagues. A city-sponsored workshop, held at the Kenilworth Community League's replacement hall in mid-November 1999, reflected on the need to activate the whole community to fight vandalism.

The wave of vandalism triggered many positive responses from the community leagues and city police. Many of the leagues became more vigilant of their security monitoring, hall rental procedures, and general safety around their playgrounds. Others entered into, or enhanced their commitment to, the EFCL-established Neighbourhood Watch program. Volunteers from the Ottewell Community League and some of its neighbours banded together to form the Ottewell Community Patrol—consisting of volunteers patrolling the neighbourhood in their own cars. Edmonton Police Service constables monitor these volunteers, who use radios to report on suspicious activities or vehicles in the area, and follow up to investigate critical incidents. A couple of drive-by shootings in their area in 2001 led to a similar program—the Mill Woods Community Patrol—in the Mill Woods and Meadows area.

Other positive outcomes included the forging in late 1999 of a closer relationship between the federation board and the senior-officer group of the Edmonton Police Service. Regular joint meetings became a norm, providing a forum for the community's voice on policing issues. On June 20, 2000, the Edmonton Journal reported acting police chief Bob Wasylyshen's commitment to a closer relationship between city police and the community leagues through the community policing strategy. Additional liaison also developed between the police and the various leagues.

EFCL executive director Bernice Neufeld and the EFCL community planning liaison, Brian McCosh, were certified in Crime Prevention Through Environmental Design (CPTED)—the process of analyzing one's facility (e.g., building, rink, community hall, or playground) to identify the risks inherent in its current layout, lighting, shrubbery, and so on. They then trained or consulted with league representatives to help make communities safer.

In May 2000, the federation voiced its concern to the city regarding the intended imposition of drainage fees on league halls and ice rinks. The conflict arose when city council, which had committed to imposing no new taxes, decided to impose new user fees including a levy on the use of sewer services. The federation objected to community leagues' designation as users (subject to the fee) for two key reasons: first, because the leagues were traditionally exempt from paying taxes, and second, because the new fees placed an undue burden on the leagues. The federation noted that the new drainage fees further exacerbated the leagues' already large utility costs.

All leagues that operated ice rinks were faced with a double whammy. On the one hand, to light their rinks, these leagues had to pay more for their power bill; on the other, they paid higher costs for the water used to flood them. The EFCL and the leagues argued the matter at length, but the cash-strapped city administration refused to budge. Council then instructed the administration to assign this fee to the landowner, namely the Community Services Department. In early 2004, the EFCL was again arguing a similar matter when the city aimed to attach a fire-hydrant fee to each water meter.

Another aspect of contention related to the way playgrounds were being developed in the city, by whom, and with what funds.[2] The long history of this matter dated back to the Gyro Club (established in 1921). The club had developed more than a dozen playgrounds in the 1920s and early 1930s. When the club's revenue decreased in the 1940s and the city recreation commission was established, responsibility for the playgrounds slowly shifted to the city. In the early 1980s, the city asked the leagues to collaborate in the development of playgrounds. Accordingly, the city provided various plans; the league selected its desired plan and raised 50 percent of the necessary funds. Each neighbourhood in the city received a one-time city grant through the Neighbourhood Park Development Program, which it could use to develop parks and playgrounds.

A 2002 review by federation and city staff of parkland and playgrounds revealed a number of interesting anomalies. In 2002, the city's share of the costs was 30 percent, with the leagues picking up the remaining 70 percent. On average, the typical playground in Edmonton costs between $300,000 and $350,000 to develop, significantly higher than in Calgary, where costs ranged from $180,000 to $210,000. Part of the difference was due to Edmonton demanding a higher safety standard than the basic Canadian Safety Association (CSA) standards and expecting the leagues to develop any parkland adjoining the playgrounds. The study concluded with a set of recommendations that included ways for the leagues and the city to support each other in ensuring safe, accessible, and resilient playgrounds for the city's residents.

As part of the City of Edmonton's budget process, in early 2003 the EFCL asked that the city review the administration of grants to community leagues. This task became the responsibility of a special committee that included five community league representatives, two from the EFCL and five from the city. The committee discussed the key grant programs (operating, maintenance /

renovation, and the emerging / merging grant), and made minor changes. A cash infusion of $200,000 partway through the process allowed for some changes to the operating grant allocations process. However, the general feeling of committee members was that any significant change to the grants process would not be worth the effort because their overall dollar value was insufficient. The committee agreed to forward a description of its status on three contentious issues, for resolution by council:

- Who should administer the grants, the EFCL or Community Services— the current administrator?
- How should the Maintenance/Renovation grant limit be assigned— by licence area or each league?
- Should the community leagues have all the necessary agreements (Licence) with the City signed?

In 2003, during the 2004 budget process, the EFCL got city council to add yet another $300,000 to the budget line for these grants, effectively doubling them in two years. City council subsequently approved the final policy document in early 2004.

Then there was the issue that simply would not go away—the city dump. On January 8, 2004, the Edmonton Journal reported that the city was again looking for a dumpsite. It was déjà vu for many citizens, who recalled the battle in the early 1980s that had established the Clover Bar landfill site. (However, with 88,000 tonnes (97,000 tons) of garbage a year delivered to the site, it will probably reach its capacity in 2010.) The Journal reported that "planners have yet to pinpoint any potential sites for a new dump here," and emphasized the urgency of starting the process of finding a suitable site.

While the federation occupied itself with these major projects and activities, the leagues continued with their own. There were many, beyond the daily fare of sports and recreation—the planning of their respective community areas, the establishment or enhancements to major community-based facilities (such as schools, libraries, hospitals, police stations and fire halls), lobbying on a multitude of issues, and generally taking a lead on issues deemed to be important for their respective areas. In many cases, community leagues banded together with their neighbouring leagues to achieve incredible success.

One such case was the thirteenth annual Canada Day celebration in Mill Woods on July 1, 2003. The event, organized by volunteers from area leagues, attracted a crowd estimated by the Edmonton Police Service to be over 40,000 people. It was the largest volunteer-organized and free Canada Day celebration in the nation. Other parts of the city had achieved their own success stories. These included the Silly Summer parade on Whyte Avenue, the annual cleanup of the river valley, and the Garbage Fairs.

From small to big, each community league has been instrumental in improving the quality of life of those who live, work, and play within greater Edmonton. Each league has left its unquestionable imprint on the well-being of all Edmonton's residents. Incredibly, the achievements of the community leagues came about through ... volunteers.

> *Victory has a hundred fathers,*
> *but defeat is an orphan.*
> — JOHN F. KENNEDY

8

Onward,
To the Future!

What do we live for,
if it is not to make life less difficult for others?

— GEORGE ELIOT

There is no limit to what can be accomplished
if it doesn't matter who gets the credit.

— RALPH WALDO EMERSON

I N 2004, EDMONTON CELEBRATED A CENTENARY AS A CITY, and the community league movement marked its eighty-seventh year of service to enhance the quality of life of Edmonton's residents.

The relationship between the city and the community leagues is distinctive in many ways. It is fundamentally focused on a participatory grassroots democratic framework that allows residents input on all civic affairs. It fosters a caring and supportive environment within and among the city's neighbourhoods. It helped Edmonton to evolve from a small town into a unique major cosmopolitan city that is unlike any other in North America or perhaps the world. Edmonton is still a city with a heart, and one that has maintained the values often seen in villages or small towns.

Interestingly, the bond between the city and the community league movement often appeared willingly, though it was frequently tested through the numerous civic issues that plagued the city and its various leagues. Yet the relationship has survived and evolved to meet the growing needs of the city's population. In the end, the relationship has nearly always been mutually beneficial.

Cake cutting ceremony on the EFCL 80th anniversary celebrations. Left to right:
Eric Mahabir, Councillor Terry Cavanagh, Ron Stauffer, Donna Fong, Ron Kuban,
Councillor Allan Bolstad, Councillor David Thiele, Don Kuchelyma. EFCL collection.

From the start, Edmonton's community leagues focused on three primary functions. These persist today. The first and perhaps the most important is to provide a forum to debate local or neighbourhood infrastructure matters. The second is to provide recreational programs and sport-related activities. The third is to develop neighbourhood facilities—such as community halls, parks, and ice rinks—to achieve these objectives. The federation's role is generally to act as a coordinating body. Despite continuous evolution to meet changing needs or demands, the leagues and their federation remained true to their original functions.

The success of Edmonton's community league movement is primarily a credit to countless volunteers. Their vision, caring spirit, commitment, and effort—often without personal recognition—have made a difference and improved the life of their fellow residents. However, credit also belongs to Edmonton's elected officials, to its bureaucrats, and its residents. Edmonton has always retained a strong sense of neighbourhood, a vibrant spirit of coop-eration, a ready willingness to volunteer when others were in need, and a compassion for one's neighbour that is rarely seen in other large cities. Edmonton's spirit of community also differs from other cities that have adopted a community league model. A significant contributor to the success of Edmonton's community league movement has been the integral relationship that the community leagues maintained with Edmonton's elected officials and its bureaucrats. This relationship provided necessary support to the league movement and reaffirmed its value. Over time, the reaffirmation became more formal and entrenched.

A recent example of this entrenchment is city council's designation of the federation as a separate line item on the city's budget and its treatment as a city board or authority. While generally positive, perhaps because of their long joint history and their partnership agreement, the close city–federation relationship is not without risk. It maintains a potential friction point with the federation and its long-time partner, the city's Community Services Department.

Over the last one hundred years, the city has gone through many cycles of growth, followed occasionally by significant economic downturns. Typically, the boom periods resulted in an incredible growth of the city's population and its infrastructure, often with the city scrambling to meet rapidly escalating infrastructure-related needs and, unfortunately, leaving many other needs unmet or only partially satisfied. The gaps in services placed great demands on the city's community leagues, which in turn scrambled to address those unmet needs, or concerns over development, or city-service inequities among the various community leagues. Predictably, the peak periods of financial boom and bust were occasions for community-based volunteers to pick up the slack and fill service-delivery gaps. Current indications point to the onset of another economic boom and perhaps another pressure point for the federation and its members.

On January 26, 2004, the Edmonton Journal reported on Syncrude Canada, operator of one of the major oil sands mines in Fort McMurray, northeast of Edmonton. The headline, "Titanium: Syncrude's Next Big Play," said it all. According to the article, Syncrude observed that the oil sands could produce a lot more than their priceless mainstay to date—oil. They could produce a variety of by-products such as "titanium, zircon and ilmenite from Syncrude waste on an industrial scale." This project is the first of its kind in Canada and is likely to generate a handsome profit for Syncrude. It is also likely to generate another kind of profit for Edmonton's service providers— another boom.

"Several projects are waiting to begin construction [in Fort McMurray] including: a $1-billion expansion of the first Shell mine at Muskeg River; the $8.5-billion Horizon Project; the $3.2-billion Long Lake project; $1.4-billion Surmont project; and a $1.2-billion bitumen upgrading addition to Petro-Canada's Edmonton refinery," reported an article in the February 6, 2004 edition of the Edmonton Journal. "More than 16,000 trades people would be required if all the projects were to go ahead at the same time."

On March 4, a Journal business section headline read: "Oilsands Growth On Pace To Double." The accompanying article reported a Canadian Energy Research Institute prediction that "barring an unexpected disaster in oil prices, Alberta oilsands production will more than double in the next 14 years, ... even if oil prices retreat from the near record highs reached so far this year."

Reportedly, the construction of Alberta's fourth oilsands mine project would require up to 3,500 workers by late 2006 and continue to demand over 2,000 people for the following five years. Being the largest and closest service-centre to Fort McMurray, Edmonton is again poised to reap the benefits.

On February 20, the Journal highlighted another of Edmonton's advantages. A recently completed KPMG survey of eleven industrialized countries found Edmonton had one of the lowest total costs of doing business—the lowest in western Canada and lower than all cities in the United States. On July 3, the Journal reported a Scotia Economics prediction that in 2005 only Alberta and BC would outpace Canada's average growth rate.

Overall, the forecast is an exciting time for Edmontonians and Albertans. The indicators provide a sense of déjà vu, a return to those periods when the oil and gas sector took off and dragged the province and Edmonton along for a ride. It was a wild one, often leading to tremendous growth, expansion, and a general sense of hope and prosperity. However, this time Edmonton is confronted by both positive and negative factors that are unique to the time. On the positive side, thanks to long-term efforts to diversify the provincial economy, the current growth involves more than just the oil and gas sectors.

A view of Edmonton.
Courtesy Edmonton Tourism/Edmonton Economic Development Corporation.

Local research institutions, notably the University of Alberta, are successfully pushing the envelope with new findings and resources, and many segments of the service sector are expanding rapidly to meet growing demand. Expansion is also noticeable in the construction industry and reflects the growth of Edmonton's population.

However, on the down side, Edmonton is no longer the only game in town. Its neighbours now confine it geographically. Consider, for example, the interaction between Edmonton and its neighbouring communities, especially Sherwood Park, St. Albert, Beaumont, and to a lesser degree, Spruce Grove. Their expansion over the years has placed their residents and businesses on the immediate outskirts of Edmonton, hemming in the city and limiting its ability to expand or to attract major industries.

However, once again and on many fronts, Edmonton is clearly outdoing itself. It has managed to attract many business enterprises because of the calibre of its workforce. Edmonton has also gained a tremendous reputation for its volunteer force, which has been an important factor in attracting many sport and artistic events. The donation of time (volunteerism) and money is alive and well right across Canada. According to Statistics Canada, in 2002 Canadians gave $5.5 billion to what they considered worthy causes. At a national level, that figure will rise to $1 trillion by the year 2022.

By its reputation, Edmonton continues to lead the way in the personal contribution of its citizens. On many occasions, their kindness has been reflected through their generous response to the needs of others at local, national, and international levels. For those at the community league level, that contribution more often involves effort and sweat equity than a simple donation of money. The contribution of Edmonton's volunteers, only briefly illustrated in earlier chapters, has made a monumental difference, repeatedly, for more than eighty-seven years.

~ ~

A recent play called A *Memory Box* highlighted the achievements of Edmonton's community league movement. Presented at the University of Alberta Timms Centre for the Arts on January 16 and 17, 2004, the play was sponsored by the Edmonton Federation of Community Leagues (EFCL) and offered completely through volunteers. Written by Mary-Ellen Perley and directed by Alex Hawkins, the play reflected the history of the federation and the community league movement. It was a fitting way to honour Edmonton's centenary, to highlight "the movement," and to illustrate its contribution to the city.

The play was a good springboard into the future, because it emphasized the enormous transformation of the federation around its core values, which, amazingly, have not changed over the last eighty-plus years. Community leagues today, like their predecessors over eight decades ago, still encourage grassroots democratic involvement by all residents—regardless of race, culture, gender, or socioeconomic conditions—on matters of local civic concern. Yet the community league movement has evolved with the times. It is poised to do so again, perhaps thanks to its recent five-year-long revitalization process.

The EFCL recently received a tremendous vote of confidence from city council—receiving its own line item on the civic budget—which gives the federation the opportunity to soar to even greater heights. Another positive condition for future growth is the slow but steady increase in the involvement of the community leagues in federation affairs. Frankly, the simple fact that the community league movement has survived the massive assault on its existence during the late 1990s is an indication of its resiliency and strength of purpose, the commitment of its countless volunteers, and the belief of elected officials in the value received through their political support of the community league movement.

Oliver Wendell Holmes stated, "Greatness is not in where we stand, but in what direction we are moving." The movement's future is sure to contain many challenges, most of which have developed to some degree over the last few decades. Primary among them is the task of meeting the needs of a growing city, and doing so amidst continued downloading of responsibilities from all orders of government. This is a major challenge for the leagues and the federation, and it exists even in good times when the demand for recreation, sports, and the necessary municipal infrastructure outstrips available resources.

The federation faces other challenges of equal significance. One such matter relates to the increasing level of risk and liability encountered by the community leagues and their volunteers, especially in the post–September 11, 2001, environment. The impact of 9/11 on the insurance industry created a quantum leap in the costs of insuring league activities, facilities, or programs. In many cases, the rising costs of insurance alone have created a major financial burden for the leagues and their fundraising efforts. Current indications are that insurance rates will not decline or level any time soon, and governments seem reluctant to set limits or provide financial relief to ratepayers. Without such sorely needed assistance, many community leagues will be forced to curtail or eliminate their activities.

One option always available to the leagues is that they work harder to raise funds and recruit (additional) volunteers to achieve league goals. However, a declining volunteer base reduces the merit of this option. The growing competition for volunteer time (and attention) is increasing exponentially as more and more organizations, even those in the public sector—schools, hospitals, social agencies, the police—seek volunteers to augment their limited resources and growing set of responsibilities. At the same time, the workload of volunteer agencies is increasing in both volume and complexity. Simply stated, there are only so many of those precious individuals, who make things happen, to go around. In addition, in time, as our population grows older, the percentage of those who volunteer their time and effort may become smaller—in part because the increasing number of seniors could generate a greater need for volunteers to assist them. On the other hand, seniors may become willing volunteers based on their experience, available time, and health.

The increasing complexity of the tasks expected to be performed by volunteers is also a major challenge. Prior to the 1990s, community league volunteers were able to perform their various roles without much training, oversight, or concern for repercussions such as liability. That is less and less the case now. The Canada Revenue Agency (formerly Revenue Canada) treats community leagues that pay for services such as ice-rink clearing or maintenance, playground supervision, or program delivery (e.g., various crafts, bike safety, dance) as "employers" and places added reporting requirements on them.

Volunteers are required to know the details of diverse and complex regulations affecting employment, taxation, human resources, occupational health and safety, and much more. League volunteers often assume roles that demand they write complex applications or reports, supervise closely the people who deliver community programs, recognize and understand liability, and protect their league and its members from a wide array of possible harm. One must remember that these folks are *volunteers*, whose primary motivation is to offer children's programs, sports, recreational activities, or help their fellow community residents. Many are ill prepared for the specialized requirements thrust upon them by government regulations or standards. The increasing complexity of their tasks causes many volunteers to become stressed, disillusioned, or burned out.

Increasingly as well, league volunteers are involved in broader and more defined linkages or partnerships. Operational relationships today are nowhere near as simple as they were a decade or two ago. Modern-day corporations and public agencies can no longer operate with total independence, and increasingly they seek partnerships to achieve their mandates. This is also the reality for the leagues already linked (perhaps intuitively) to the schools, hospitals, major social agencies, and other public agencies that operate in their area. The trend is continuing to grow more popular, with partnerships becoming more demanding and more complex.

Another major challenge for the leagues is the issue of volunteer management. To be fair, the whole process of volunteer management is slowly working itself into the radar screen of the not-for-profit sector. It is a reality that will not disappear, because modern life has become more complex and requires structure;

therefore, leagues find themselves increasingly involved with the process of recruitment (including the screening of volunteers), orientation, training, supervision, recognition, discipline, and dismissal, than ever before. Nevertheless, the trend is a benefit for the leagues, as it encourages them to become more efficient and systematic in how they conduct their affairs. Increasingly, like many businesses and other enterprises, the leagues are expected to be more open, more efficient, and more accountable in their financial affairs.

To achieve their complex goals, community leagues have to make contact with a diversity of public sector agencies. This trend will likely continue to escalate, despite city administration's effort to funnel all league requests or queries through one contact agency—the Community Services Department. One cause for this trend is the increasing reliance of the leagues on external agencies or non-traditional funding sources. Another reason is the community leagues' growing frustration with what they see as an effort to filter or manage their message.

Clearly, community leagues that are more sophisticated or experienced demand to speak directly to those who can provide desired information or action. The leagues are also frustrated with their growing financial constraints. The currently high demand for additional and more diverse sources of funding, especially for league programs, will continue to increase. This is a consequence of the limited ability of the municipal government to fund all the programs and services demanded of it by its public.

Nevertheless, the city and the province have to recognize the value-added return their grants are providing the City of Edmonton and the Alberta Capital Region, and commit sustainable funds that will allow the community league movement to develop and deliver its valuable services. Failure to do so places these programs and services in great jeopardy, and risks an escalation of the direct cost to the city (by providing these necessary services through its own staff).

The federation board and staff face a monumental challenge—to coordinate, lead, or support the community leagues in a future that is bound to be more complex and demanding. Micromanagement is out as a viable alternative, even if permitted by the leagues. There are simply not enough resources at federation (versus league) level to micromanage league activities or sport programs.

The EFCL's current office.
EFCL collection.

Because of the ever-increasing complexity of the growing federation, where many issues could potentially splinter the membership into opposing camps, consensus building has to be the modus operandi. As a result, the governance of the federation must also evolve to reflect a growing involvement by the leagues in federation affairs. Ultimately, the federation exists to serve its community leagues; however, the former cannot achieve its Herculean task without the active support of the latter.

Life continues to evolve and place increasingly complex demands on our organizations, our community, and ourselves. Thomas Jefferson stated, "I like the dreams of the future better than the history of the past." The long-ago dream—of making community life a little better for the local residents—has materialized successfully beyond the dreams of those who initiated it. For over eighty years, the dream has continued, implemented day after day by a steady stream of countless volunteers. Each small venture added to a tapestry that created a city; each village-like community league added to the formation of a cosmopolitan city.

Over the last eighty-plus years, Edmonton's community league movement has undergone an amazing transformation. At its start, the movement focused

EFCL board member Donna Fong (left) and EFCL volunteers participate in the Silly Summer Parade along Whyte Avenue, Canada Day 2002. EFCL collection.

on quality-of-life issues at the neighbourhood level, first on infrastructure issues but soon including the development and operation of recreational space such as playgrounds and rinks. In time, the community leagues began to deliver recreational programs, soon coupled with sports programs. These grew rapidly, and the federation started to coordinate the delivery of various sports programs. With the creation by the city of district-level recreational facilities starting in the 1960s, the federation and its leagues divested themselves of the coordination of sports and reverted to the provision of recreational programs. Throughout their existence, the leagues remained fervent advocates on behalf of their neighbourhood and the issues that affected their quality of life.

Chinese philosopher Lao Tzu noted, "A journey of a thousand miles begins with one step." Although it came through thousands of such miles, the federation, its 145 community leagues, and their community league movement are now ready again to continue their journey. They have already demonstrated their determination, caring nature, stamina, ingenuity, adaptability, and fearlessness, in spite of both internal and external foes. These qualities will help the movement stay its course and continue to make Edmonton a place to call home.

Amazingly, while the movement remained flexible and adapted to countless changes over the years, its values remained unchanged. Its volunteers espouse these values, almost on an intuitive basis. As a result, current league programs and services clearly reflect these values as core themes.

The community leagues serve at grassroots level, and the first volunteer most children in Edmonton are likely to meet is one from their community league. These volunteers serve as critical role models for future generations. Thanks to the effort of its thousands of volunteers, Edmonton's movement of integrated "urban villages" is strong. It will not easily dismantle, and it will continue to make Edmonton a special place to call home.

*Success is not built
on what we accomplish for ourselves.
Its foundation lies in what we do for others.*
— COMEDIAN DANNY THOMAS

List of Current Leagues

	COMMUNITY LEAGUE	EST. IN	COMMENTS
001	Alberta Avenue	1922	
002	Aldergrove	1977	
003	Allendale	1955	from 1920–55, part of Parkallen
004	Argyll	1956	
005	Aspen Gardens	1966	
006	Athlone	1958	
007	Avonmore	1957	
008	Balwin	1962	
009	Bannerman	1980	
010	Baturyn	1980	
011	Beacon Heights	1965	
012	Belgravia	1954	
013	Bellevue	1920	
014	Belmead	1984	
015	Belvedere	1925	
016	Beverly Heights	1949	
017	Blue Quill	1979	
018	Bonnie Doon	1918	
019	Boyle Street	1946	
020	Britannia-Youngstown	1959	
021	Brookview	1993	
022	Burnewood	1981	
023	Caernarvon	1974	

	COMMUNITY LEAGUE	EST. IN	COMMENTS
024	Calder	1920	
025	Callingwood-Lymburn	1979	
026	Canora	1949	
027	Capilano	1958	
028	Carlisle	1977	
029	Central McDougall	1923	
030	Cloverdale	1920	
031	Crestwood	1917	
	Cromdale	1925	see Parkdale (#104)
032	Cumberland-Oxford	2002	
033	Delton	1961	
034	Delwood	1965	
035	Dovercourt	1955	
036	Downtown Edmonton Community Association (DECA)	1999	
037	Duggan	1971	
038	Dunluce	1978	
039	Eastwood	1923	
040	Edmonton Garrison	1992	
041	Ellerslie	1962	
042	Elmwood	1964	
043	Elmwood Park	1946	
044	Empire Park	1968	
045	Ermineskin	1978	
046	Evansdale	1971	
047	Evergreen	1982	
	Fountain Lake	1987	see The Meadows (#126)
048	Forest/Terrace Heights	1920	
049	Fraser	1982	
050	Fulton Place	1958	
051	Garneau	1921	
052	Glengarry	1964	
053	Glenora	1949	

	COMMUNITY LEAGUE	EST. IN	COMMENTS
054	Glenwood	1939	
055	Gold Bar	1960	
056	Grandview Heights	1961	
057	Greenfield	1967	
058	Grovenor	1952	
059	Hairsine	1980	
060	Hazeldean	1955	
061	High Park	1959	
062	Highlands	1921	
063	Holyrood	1956	
064	Homesteader	1976	
065	Horse Hill	1972	
066	Idylwylde	1955	
067	Inglewood	1950	
068	Jasper Park	1951	
069	Kenilworth	1964	
070	Kensington	1960	
071	Kilkenny	1970	
072	Killarney	1960	
073	King Edward Park	1921	
074	Knottwood	1977	
075	La Perle	1983	
076	Lago Lindo	1983	
077	Lakewood	1978	
078	Lansdowne	1967	
079	Lauderdale	1957	
080	Laurier Heights	1958	
081	Leefield	1973	
082	Lendrum	1962	
083	Lessard	1982	
084	Lewis Estates	1994	
085	Londonderry	1968	
086	Lorelei-Beaumaris	1978	
087	Lynnwood	1960	

	COMMUNITY LEAGUE	EST. IN	COMMENTS
088	Malmo	1965	
089	Mayfield	1957	
090	McCauley	1935	
091	McKernan	1932	
092	McLeod	1970	
093	McQueen	1955	
094	Meadowlark	1959	
095	Meadows, The	1987	first established as Fountain Lake
096	Millhurst	1979	
097	Montrose	1951	
098	Newton	1954	
099	North Glenora	1953	
100	North Millbourne	1975	
101	Northmount	1971	
102	Ogilvie Ridge	1997	
103	Oliver	1922	
	Ormsby	1981	see Willowby (#138)
104	Ottewell	1961	
105	Parkallen	1920	
106	Parkdale	1921	joined Cromdale in 1986
107	Parkview	1956	
108	Pleasantview	1946	
109	Prince Charles	1954	
110	Prince Rupert	1962	
111	Queen Alexandra	1962	
112	Queen Mary Park	1952	
113	Ridge, The	1994	
114	Ridgewood	1982	
115	Rio Terrace	1960	
116	Ritchie	1922	
117	Riverbend	1970	
118	Riverdale	1920	
119	Rossdale	1922	
120	Rosslyn	1961	

	COMMUNITY LEAGUE	EST. IN	COMMENTS
121	Royal Gardens	1968	
122	Sherbrooke	1948	
	Sherwood	1949	amalgamated in 1985 to form West Jasper Sherwood (#132)
123	South Clareview	1977	
124	Southwood	1980	
125	Spruce Avenue	1918	
126	Steele Heights	1967	
127	Strathcona (Centre)	1918	
128	Strathearn	1953	
129	Summerlea	1984	
	Terrace Heights	1966	now officially with Forest Heights
130	Thorncliff	1971	
131	Twin Brooks	2002	
132	Twin Parks	1977	
133	Wedgewood Ravine	1990	
134	Wellington Park	1958	
	West Jasper Place	1950	joined Sherwood in 1985 to form West Jasper Sherwood
135	West Jasper Sherwood	1985	
136	West Meadowlark	1965	
137	Westmount	1951	
138	Westridge / Wolf Willow	1977	
139	Westview Village	1985	
140	Westwood	1951	
141	Willowby	1981	first established as Ormsby (name changed in 1986)
142	Windsor Park	1947	
143	Woodcroft	1957	
144	Woodvale	1980	
145	Yellowbird East	1981	

APPENDIX 2

About
Area Councils

These summaries are based on submissions by each area council
currently in operation in Edmonton.

AREA COUNCIL I

Area Council 1 has been active for over thirty years and includes the communities of Athlone, Calder, Lauderdale, Rosslyn, Kensington, and Wellington Park. Close to $1 million generated by the area council has been allocated to local projects and programs, thereby enhancing the quality of life for the area's residents.

More specifically, funding has been provided in four important areas. The first is the Grand Trunk Complex, which includes an arena and a swimming pool. Area Council 1 convinced the city and the provincial government to provide the necessary funds to develop a major family-oriented swimming pool. This project was Edmonton's first major facility that involved the area council in its complete planning process and construction. The area council had a major involvement in the operations plan and is still involved in the facility's operation.

After the facility's pool opened on September 12, 1976, the area council reviewed operations to identify shortfalls. Attendance was low, indicating some improvement and additions were needed to make the facility more attractive. Some enhancements were made, including upgrades to the common area and the addition of a hot tub, steam room, a weight and exercise room, an air-conditioned conference room, a fully-equipped kitchen, and a viewing room. The area is available for rent and is often used for children's parties and the like. The council also furnished the common area and the conference room, and funded improvements to the player boxes and the official box.

A second area of funding is in sports teams. Over the past twenty years, the area council has provided funding, including some operating expenses, for more than twenty-five youth organizations, including hockey, basketball, soccer, and ringette.

A third area of funding relates to both capital and program financial support for a variety of not-for-profit organizations in and outside the council area. These include: Stollery Children Hospital, Compassion House, Burn Unit, Alberta Cancer Foundation, STARS air ambulance, Partners for Youth Outreach Society, Calder Seniors Drop-in Centre, Boy Scouts, Alberta Sports Hall of Fame, Ron Hayter Women's Bursary, Ron Hayter Men's Bursary, and Air One Project (the EPS helicopter). The council also contributed over $36,000 and countless volunteer hours to the Boysdale Camp Foundation.

The fourth area of contribution by the council involves annual funding for a number of organizations and projects, including the Edmonton Christmas Bureau, Santa Anonymous, Poppy Fund, Neighbourhood Police Station, Bissell Centre, WIN House, and many more. As well, the council has been active in such issues as zoning, roadway and area development, tree removal, and recreation facilities.

AREA COUNCIL 2

Established in June 1966, the Edmonton North District Area Council 2 is a volunteer, non-profit society. It represents a number of community interest groups and six community leagues: Balwin, Belvedere, Delwood, Glengarry, Killarney, and Rosslyn. During the area council's early years, its main focus was on the sponsorship and coordination of hockey programs for its members. Reflecting the growth of its community, the council grew and evolved in its mandate, and in February 1976, the society was incorporated as the Edmonton North District Area Council 2. Over the next decade, the communities of Bannerman, Evergreen, Fraser, Hairsine, Homesteader, Horse Hill, Kirkness, and South Clareview, as well as a number of new community interest groups, joined the council. With the direction of elected representatives, the council identified and pursued mutual issues and concerns that went beyond community league boundaries.

As the number and size of the communities in the area grew, so did their need. One such need related to a recreational centre in the area. In September

1982, Area Council 2 formed an advisory committee that would see through a proposal for and the development of a recreation centre in Castle Downs. Within a few years it also became apparent that the needs of area residents would be better served through two area councils. This triggered the establishment, in June 1987, of a second area council—the Clareview Area Council, which was supported by Area Council 2 in the planning for the Clareview Recreation Centre.

In May 1985, the area council was approached to provide needed equipment for the O'Leary swimming pool. It was the beginning of several enhancements made through the support of the area council and its many volunteers. Plans were made and funds raised to add in 1987 a whirlpool and sauna at the pool. Two years later a new parking lot was also added. In November 1993, a $1.2-million building renovation was completed at the site, adding a wading and teaching pool, multipurpose room, office, and a boardroom. In 1999 a new slide was added, and in 2003 construction began on a new fitness room. To date, Area Council 2 has raised over $2 million for upgrades to the centre.

Area Council 2 has also addressed other needs of the area's residents besides recreation. Recognizing the traffic-safety hazards in the area, the council purchased Neighbourhood Patrol identity signs for the six community leagues it serves. Also, as a long-term advocate for the availability of health care services in the area, in January 1999 the council welcomed the opening of a public health and family medicine unit. Later that year, in September, it welcomed the opening of the Northeast Emergency Health Centre.

The successes of Area Council 2 are directly attributed to the contribution of hundreds of dedicated and hard-working volunteers. Over the last twenty-eight years the council has taken pride in celebrating these volunteers through an annual recognition banquet and award ceremony. The council continues to encourage and facilitate citizen participation through discussion, planning, and action on issues that affect the area's residents.

AREA COUNCIL 17

Area Council 17 was formed in 1975 as a non-profit organization under the Society Act of Alberta. It is a voluntary organization made up of representatives from the seven community leagues within its boundaries—Steele Heights, McLeod, Kilkenny, Londonderry, Northmount, Evansdale, and Lago Lindo.

Also included are representatives of schools, organizations, agencies, and interested individuals who live within the area, which is bounded by the city limits on the north, 97th Street on the west, 137th Avenue on the south, and Manning Freeway on the east.

The council encourages citizen participation in its consideration, discussion, and action on issues affecting area residents, its liaison between community, government agencies, and its work toward the betterment of the community. Area Council 17 takes great pride in the way that it is structured to represent area residents and to encourage them to get involved.

Issues faced by the area include planning and development, landfill construction (turned down due to environmental concerns), lack of recreational facilities (parks, playgrounds, and sport facilities), and transportation (road development). Some of the council's successes include:

- construction of the first water park in the Edmonton area
- construction of shale ball diamonds
- financial contribution toward local programs (such as Christmas hampers, Neighbourhood Watch, and Ronald McDonald House) and facilities (such as the Castle Downs YMCA and Londonderry Pool)
- support for local agencies and schools
- provision of Area Swim (free swim) and ice programs (e.g., Can Skate, Learn to Skate, and shinny hockey)

Much of the money contributed by Area Council 17 comes from the voluntary effort of numerous individuals who work bingos and casinos. Their contribution is becoming more and more difficult to secure, while demands for services and contributions are increasing. The area council is working hard to overcome this predicament, and is proud of its achievements to date.

CASTLE DOWNS RECREATION SOCIETY
(A.K.A. AREA RECREATION COUNCIL NO. 20)
The Castle Downs Recreation Society (CDRS) is made up of the six community leagues within the Castle Downs area: Baturyn, Caernarvon, Carlisle, Cumberland-Oxford, Dunluce, and Lorelei-Beaumaris. It represents the area west of 97th Street to the St. Albert Trail and north of 137th Avenue, which in 2004 included a fast-growing population (in the north and west) of over 40,000.

The CDRS was informally established in 1983 as a subcommittee of Area Recreation Council 1. Area Council 1, the first area council in the Edmonton Federation of Community Leagues, was composed of six long-established leagues south of 137th Avenue: Athlone, Calder, Kensington, Lauderdale, Rosslyn, and Wellington Park. The Castle Downs leagues began to organize in the late 1970s and early 1980s, and were welcomed into Area Council 1, working as a subcommittee of Area Council 1 from 1983 through the mid-1980s to meet the growing need for major recreation facilities in the Castle Downs area. In 1987, the five leagues in Castle Downs formed the Castle Downs Recreation Society to aggressively pursue the needs inherent to the Castle Downs area.

The CDRS operated as a member of Area Council 1 until 1993, when it established itself as a separate entity and was recognized by the EFCL as Area Recreation Council No. 20. This allowed the CDRS to focus on the increasing needs and issues of its 30,000-plus residents. The experience gained in Area 1, combined with the enthusiastic and dedicated volunteers in Castle Downs, provided the energy and drive to achieve great things. For example, over its twenty-year history the CDRS has invested over $1 million in the Castle Downs area. In addition to being involved in the area's community issues, the CDRS has worked with other organizations on issues of importance to north Edmonton. It has achieved a long list of accomplishments relating to both programs and facilities.

The CDRS lobbied for and helped design the Castle Downs Recreation Centre. Work on the centre started in 1983. When it opened in September 1989, the society donated $50,000 to furnish it. A few years later, through a unique partnership that CDRS established with the YMCA, the City of Edmonton, and the Southwest Area Council, two new family-related YMCA facilities were built in Edmonton. One of them—the Castle Downs YMCA—opened in June 1998 after five years of construction and an infusion of more than $300,000 from the area council.

A year earlier, 1997, saw the completion of the Castle Downs Water Park at the west end of Castle Downs Park. The project was a team effort by the CDRS, which raised about $450,000; students from Mary Butterworth Junior High, who designed the park; and volunteers, who built it. The CDRS also partnered with the city to build an indoor waterslide at Grand Trunk Pool, contributing $20,000 toward the capital cost of $60,000. It also participated in the North East Area Councils Association to pursue a regional health centre, and in 2004 opened a $500,000 skateboard park. All in all, the CDRS's total financial investment in Castle Downs is in the order of $1.3 million.

Additionally, the CDRS has made significant contribution to many of the area's programs. These include the Annual Castle Downs Hockey School, free Saturday evening swim for community league members at the YMCA, free Sunday afternoon swim for community league members at Grand Trunk Pool, free Saturday skate for community league members at the Castle Downs Recreation Centre, the summer playground program at the Castle Downs Water Park, and the summer skateboard park in the parking lot by the Castle Downs Recreation Centre. Each year, the CDRS hosts a Canada Day and Klondike Days celebration at the Castle Downs Water Park. Various other programs have also been offered over the years (e.g., teen dances, pre-school), and countless donations made to various community groups on an application basis. The CDRS estimates that its total annual investment in programs is $10,000, and its total investment to date over $100,000.

Time and again, the area council has facilitated public discussion on issues of concern for the area's residents. Such issues included the women's prison proposed for the area (but turned down based on feedback), construction of separate and public high schools in the area, establishment of a close working relationship with Canada Lands Corporation to develop an innovative new neighbourhood in the Griesbach area (the land formerly held by the Canadian Armed Forces).

The Castle Downs Recreation Society holds its Annual Volunteer Appreciation Night and numerous fundraising activities—bingos, casinos, auctions, a variety show, a fashion show—that generate an annual income of about $50,000. The CDRS has a proud history that will be carried into the future. As always, this future will be built on the commitment and support of the community leagues in the area and the dedication of many volunteers.

CENTRAL AREA COUNCIL OF COMMUNITY LEAGUES

The Central Area Council of Community Leagues (CACCL) was created as an offshoot of the Southwest Area Council (SWAC). The northernmost communities of SWAC determined that, on some issues, the interests of the developing communities in southwest Edmonton were diversely different from those of the more established neighbourhoods in the north. For example, whereas newer communities had concerns over the creation of infrastructure, these northern communities were concerned with maintenance and rehabilitation of their existing infrastructure. Often, the interests of the southern communities were diametrically opposed to those in the north, and transportation became a pivotal issue. The southern communities wanted faster access to core areas which, potentially, meant enlarging roads through the northern communities.

Because of these differences, a series of meetings was held with a number of northern communities of SWAC to determine the level of interest in a proposal to form an area council for these older communities. Some, such as Grandview Heights, did not wish to proceed with a separate area council; others were interested but not necessarily committed. On June 12, 1995, the communities of Belgravia, Garneau, Lendrum, McKernan, Parkallen, Pleasantview, Queen Alexandra, and Strathcona Centre held the first formal meeting to discuss the creation of a new area council. Although invited to the meeting, representatives from the communities of Allendale, Empire Park, and Windsor Park were unable to attend.

Following this initial meeting, the communities met on an informal basis until April 11, 1996, when the CACCL's founding meeting was held at the Queen Alexandra Community Hall. At the meeting, the bylaws were adopted. CACCL was registered under the Societies Act on April 26, 1996, with the following adopted purpose:

> The Central Area Council of Community Leagues will provide a forum
> to address the concerns and aspirations of inner city neighbourhoods
> in south Edmonton. The Council will foster discussion and promote
> action to ensure the continued viability of member communities.

The CACCL's initial league members included Allendale, Belgravia, McKernan, Parkallen, Pleasantview, Queen Alexandra, Strathcona Centre, and Windsor Park. The council became a vehicle for the discussion of topics significant to its member communities, including 106th Street, 114th Street, truck routes, the Transportation Master Plan, video lottery terminals (VLTs), Plan Edmonton, Mature Neighborhood Overlay, the University of Alberta expansion (especially with respect to the south campus), and various other development

In 2000, the Central Area Council of Community Leagues (CACCL) became involved as an intervener before the Alberta Energy and Utility Board in the matter of EPCOR Utilities' proposed expansion of the Rossdale power plant. This came about because, in the fall of 1999, Edo Nyland, president of the Windsor Park Community League, and Elaine Solez, president of the CACCL, attended a forum about electricity organized by concerned citizens and politicians. Topics included the city's consideration of selling EPCOR, the impact of deregulation, and EPCOR's proposal to expand the Rossdale power-generating station.

It was clear at the forum that the expansion was a city-wide issue as it would affect the central river valley for decades to come. It was also clear that several CACCL member leagues would be directly affected by the expansion plans, as two overlooked the plant and four bordered the high-pressure gas line that needed to be installed by ATCO. In addition, if Rossdale residents were the only ones to oppose the plans, they would be seen as NIMBYs ("Not in my back-yards").

The involvement of the CACCL (as well as the Rossdale Community League and the EFCL) as intervener was an extensive exercise. Status as intervener had to be established, lawyers and experts had to be retained, and materials to present to the Alberta Energy and Utility Board had to be prepared. The intervention of the three community league organizations, the EFCL, ConCerv (Concerned Citizens for Edmonton's River Valley), and a host of cultural, historical, and preservation groups was coordinated. Together they made a very credible presentation in fall 2000, covering a vast number of topics: environmental concerns (air and water), archaeological and historical significance, the planning history of the site, and property values.

While the Alberta Energy and Utility Board approved the application to expand in spring 2001, they also referred to Alberta Community Development the matter of the historical significant of the Low Pressure Plant Building, most of which was going to be demolished to expand the power plant. In the summer of 2001, the

CACCL, EFCL, and Rossdale Community League (among other organizations) participated in a subsequent review conducted by the Alberta Historical Resources Board. Following the review, the minister of community development designated the building a provincial historic resource. This designation effectively halted the expansion of the power plant.

Part of the effort by the CACCL and the EFCL on this issue was preparing a position paper for city council on decommissioning the Rossdale power plant and adapting the buildings as an attraction for the public. As a result, in October 2002, city council held a hearing on the future of the power plant, and EPCOR is developing a long-range plan for the plant.

---

issues in the area. However, the most significant project undertaken by CACCL involved the Rossdale power plant.

In addition, CACCL has administered a community swim program at the Scona Pool. Although all the participant leagues are not members of CACCL, the program has been administered exclusively by CACCL.

On October 7, 1998, the Empire Park Community League became a member of the CACCL. In 2003, the Rossdale Community League also became a member, marking the first time a community located on the north side of the North Saskatchewan River had joined the CACCL. The council continues to play an important role in advocacy on behalf of its members and in sharing information with its leagues. It has gained a reputation for being one of the most active area councils in the new millennium.

SOUTH EAST COMMUNITY LEAGUE ASSOCIATION

Incorporated in 2000, the South East Community League Association (SECLA) is the youngest of the area councils. It is located in southeast Edmonton, and its membership includes ten community leagues: Avonmore, Capilano, Forest/Terrace Heights, Fulton Place, Gold Bar, Holyrood, Idylwylde, Kenilworth, Ottewell, and Strathearn.

Despite its youth, SECLA has made significant contributions to its area and the city. Its achievements include:

- approval of the Southeast Area Plan—the largest community-driven planning document in the city of Edmonton—by city council in 1998, and continued involvement in updating the plan with input from the leagues and the area's senior citizens
- ongoing review and commentary on planning and transportation issues
- completion in 2003 of a major international environmental project, "The South East Community Leagues Association Green Map For 2003"
- sponsorship of a community newspaper, the *Southeast Voice*, delivered ten times a year to 14,000 area households
- development of a multi-use recreation park for area youth

Demographically, the residents of SECLA communities represent an older population and include over twice the city's average number of seniors.

MILL WOODS PRESIDENTS' COUNCIL

In many regards, the young community of Mill Woods in Edmonton's southeast corner became an incredible role model for the EFCL, which, according to the *Edmonton Examiner* (December 12, 1983), encouraged others to follow the Mill Woods approach. The organization in Mill Woods started as an area council, but within a few years, in late 1983, it had transformed into a community council. This council, established as a non-partisan agency that presented its community's concerns to all levels of government, was and continues to be an amazing enterprise with steadily increasing strength in capacity and reach, when many other area councils have wavered or dissolved.

The Mill Woods Community Council, now known as the Mill Woods Presidents' Council (MWPC), has many interesting aspects. From the start it focused its efforts on coordinating the voices and desires of community leagues in the area (see sidebar for background on Mill Woods), which felt severely isolated from the rest of the city. (An industrial belt and a major transportation route, to the west along 91st Street and to the north along Whitemud Drive, separated the area from the rest of Edmonton.) To the east and the south lay only farmland, ready to be developed. Moreover, as each of the area leagues was established, it quickly realized that its residents had no recreation facilities or infrastructure. Given that they were too distant to access neighbouring league facilities or programs, Mill Woods residents quickly realized that they must become self-reliant. (In fact, their situation was similar to that experienced by the new leagues of the 1920s and 1930s.)

Mill Woods's urgent need for a strong voice at city hall and its need to efficiently use limited volunteer resources led to the creation of its community council. Established in late 1977, the Mill Woods Presidents' Council (MWPC) had a mandate to "bring cohesion to the community through the strengths of the community league organizations, and to enhance and enrich the lives of the citizens of Mill Woods." The council soon proved extremely valuable in gaining the attention of the city's elected officials and administration. However, to the community's credit, its people were also ready to step up to the plate and do their share to secure needed resources or facilities.

Over time, the MWPC established or supported a variety of committees including Mill Woods Hockey (1978), Mill Woods Soccer (1979), multicultural initiatives, and the Anti-Poverty Roundtable. Other committees operated by the MWPC have been responsible for the annual Canada Day celebration in Mill Woods, the Mill Woods Day celebrations, and the operations of the Mill Woods Newsletter, delivered to all area residents.

Among the community council's major achievements was the creation in the late 1970s of the Mill Woods Cultural and Recreational Facilities Association (MCARFA). A wing of existing community leagues, MCARFA's mandate was to develop recreational and cultural facilities within the community. With its elected board of directors nearly always consisting of community league members, MCARFA maintained ongoing and close liaison with the community council and its member leagues.

Once established, MCARFA set out to raise money toward a district-level recreational centre. In time, it joined forces with the City of Edmonton and the Mill Woods Presidents' Council to complete the recreational centre earlier and in a more expanded form than anticipated. MCARFA was also instrumental in the establishment of the eighteen-hole Mill Woods Golf Course (opened in 1989) and the creation of Jackie Parker Park (in the late 1990s). MCARFA has also been involved in the refurbishing of the public tennis courts, the creation of a running track south of the Mill Woods Recreational Centre, and most recently the construction of the Mill Woods Skate Board Park.

The area now known as Mill Woods was, during the early 1800s, inhabited by the Papaschase First Nation. When the reserve was forsaken for other localities, the area became part of a large agricultural segment known as Bruederfeld. Many settlers, mostly from Russia and Germany, arrived in the late 1800s to settle the area of Mill Woods. They ran a communal farm and had many ties to Bruederheim and the Moravian Church.

In 1969, to meet the growing needs for affordable housing, the City of Edmonton began annexing lands in the Bruederfeld area. In 1970, in conjunction with Alberta Housing, the city put into action a development plan and began purchasing nearly 24 square kilometres (9 square miles) of land—over 2,330 hectares (4,425 acres)—from private owners in southeast Edmonton for what would become Mill Woods. It received its name from the Mill Creek, which drained the area.

The new community, highlighted in the 1971 *Mill Woods Development Concept* report, was intended "to create a showpiece of new urban growth that would be achieved by incorporating sound principles of social, economic and physical planning." It was designed for low- to middle-income families and developed from scratch to be a community unto itself. Residential construction in the area began in 1972 and accelerated through the 1970s. (Land, sold at relatively low prices, was in great demand and created a mad rush of would-be purchasers, some of whom camped out in front of the land sale office.) In the early 1980s, growth slowed due to a downturn in the economy, but accelerated again later that decade. By 1987 the community numbered 65,000 residents and in 2003 more than 86,000. (A current joke in Mill Woods is that if it separated from Edmonton, it would easily become Alberta's third largest city.) Amazingly, the Mill Woods population reflects an incredible diversity of ethnicity and religions—representing over 85 percent of the world's cultures and languages.

The growth of Mill Woods has greatly benefited Edmonton. Revenues from its development have been invested in the Mill Woods Reserve Fund, which provided $118 million to finance a

number of important citywide initiatives. The fund has loaned the City of Edmonton money to purchase Century Place, Chancery Hall, and the new city hall.

The Mill Woods Presidents' Council's newly elected president in 1984, Brian Sugiyama, was the outgoing president of the Ridgewood Community League and a recreation consultant with the provincial recreation and parks department. He began implementing a consultant's report that recommended the council establish a guidebook for the leagues to assist them in the conduct of their affairs.

EFCL
Code of Ethics

PREAMBLE

The Code of Ethics consists of moral obligations aimed at upholding the dignity and integrity of community leagues within the Edmonton Federation of Community Leagues, ("the Society"). It attempts to define those obligations that benefit all leagues and also areas that should be avoided. In general, the code is designed to assist the operating efficiency of all individual leagues and of the practical interpretation of the aims and objectives of the community league philosophy.

ARTICLE 1

The first duty of a community league must be to strictly observe its constitution and by-laws as registered under The Societies Act RSA 1980 c S–18 equally and without regard to race, creed, colour, religion, ethnic origin, sex or political affiliation.

ARTICLE 2

A community league should restrict membership to those residents living within the boundaries of that league as designated by the Society and the City of Edmonton.

ARTICLE 3

Where a neighbourhood does not operate as a community league, then the nearest neighbouring community league may enrol residents from that neighbourhood as members or associate members of their league.

ARTICLE 4

Each community league must honour other league memberships for the remainder of the current membership year with regard to members moving their place of residence from one league to another.

ARTICLE 5

Where enrolment capacity permits, each community league will admit members from other community leagues to all programs for a uniform admission fee and without an additional membership charge.

ARTICLE 6

Each community league should support and strengthen the Society in a true community spirit.

ARTICLE 7

Each community league should always endeavour to improve relationships among individual leagues, the Society and the City of Edmonton.

ARTICLE 8

Leagues should encourage and support inter-league communication and cooperation, particularly in shared programs.

ARTICLE 9

Each community league should be prepared to help new leagues with advice or resources in order for the new leagues to become established and successful.

ARTICLE 10

Each league should hold regular meetings to which officers should conscientiously attend as well as attending the Society meetings.

ARTICLE 11

Each community league should maintain a complete and accurate record of all its business and comply with the requirements of the Societies Act in respect of its Annual General Meetings and extraordinary resolutions.

ARTICLE 12

Each league should encourage fair play among its members in all activities. Each league should further observe that it is participation and enjoyment that counts far more than winning.

ARTICLE 13

Community leagues should always observe and respect municipal, provincial and federal laws of the land.

ARTICLE 14

Each league should conduct its business in a manner that is open, ethical, in compliance with its by-laws, and which avoids a perceived conflict of interest.

Notes

FROM FUR TRADERS TO BUREAUCRATS

1. For an extensive history of the Hudson's Bay Company, see Peter Newman's *Company of Adventurers*.

2. For a flavour of the Klondike period, read Pierre Berton's account in *Klondike: The Life and Death of the Last Great Gold Rush*.

3. For a pictorial and narrative history of Strathcona, check out Ken Tingley's *The Strathcona Dream*.

4. Tony Cashman's book *Edmonton Exhibition: The First Hundred Years* provides a wonderful history of the Exhibition as well as Edmonton's evolution.

5. Robert Brown and Ramsay Cook provide an informative narrative of Canada's history in *Canada: 1896–1921*. It's a worthy read. So is the series *Alberta in the Twentieth Century* edited by Paul Bunner, especially Volume 1, *The Great West Before 1900*, and Volume 2, *The Birth of the Province*.

THE COMMUNITY GIVES A VOICE

1. An extensive coverage of the period may be found in Volume 3, *The Boom and the Bust*, Volume 4, *The Great War and its Consequences*, and Volume 5, *Brownlee and the Triumph of Populism*, of the Paul Bunner (ed.) series *Alberta in the Twentieth Century*.

2. For a broad history of Edmonton, especially the area around the Rossdale power-generating plant, read the February 2004 report by Commonwealth Historic Resource Management titled *Rossdale Historical Land Use Study*. It covers Edmonton's early history and provides a detailed description of its land use. Valuable maps and diagrams are included.

3. For specific details about the growth of the King Edward Park and district, read John Chalmer's version of the book titled *Looking Back: King Edward Park and District*.

4. Canada's history of World War I is well documented. Among the better sources are the *Canadian Expeditionary Force 1914–1918* by Colonel G. W. L. Nicholson, *Marching as to War* by Pierre Berton, and *Canada's Soldiers: The Military History of an Unmilitary People* by George Stanley.

5. The 1915 flood in Edmonton and the rich history of the Riverdale area are captured by Allan Shute and Margaret Fortier in *Riverdale: From Fraser Flats to Edmonton Oasis*.

6   For details about the formation of the EFCL and community-specific history, read *Volunteers* by Vaughn Bowler and Michael Wanchuk.

7   For more in-depth coverage of the EFCL's formation, visit the *Edmonton Bulletin* and *Edmonton Journal* from that era, or the historical files held by the EFCL (available online at www.efcl.org).

COMMUNITY SPIRIT IN DEPRESSION AND WAR

1   A detailed history of Edmonton during this period is found in James MacGregor's account, *Edmonton: A History*.

2   Wheat prices quoted in the early part of this chapter are from Gilpin's *Edmonton: Gateway to the North*.

3   For a history of the Depression era across the prairies, see Broadfoot, *Ten Lost Years*. His book provides a unique flavour of the era through the stories of those who experienced it.

4   The quote from Mayor Douglas is from Gilpin (*Edmonton*, p. 149), who provides a broad treatment of the events of the day.

5   There are countless sources on Canada's involvement during World War II. Some of the more official and interesting records include: *The Canadian Army 1939–1945* and *Six Years of War*, both by Colonel C. P. Stacey.

6   For a history of the Edmonton Exhibition, check out Tony Cashman's 1979 book, *Edmonton Exhibition: The First Hundred Years*.

7   For a good read, see Volume 8, *The War That United the Province*, of the Paul Bunner (ed.) series, *Alberta in the Twentieth Century*.

BLACK GOLD, ROUGHNECKS, AND A BOOMING COMMUNITY

1   For more detail about post–World War II residential development, check out J. P. Smith's chapter titled "Planning for Residential Growth Since the 1940s" (pp. 243–55) in Bob Hesketh and Frances Swyripa's 1995 book, *Edmonton: The Life of a City*.

2   Donald Creighton's *The Forked Road* provides an informative view of Canada's history during this period.

3   Paul Bunner (ed.) provides a great account of the era in the series *Alberta in the Twentieth Century*. See Volume 9, *Leduc, Manning and the Age of Prosperity*, as well as Volume 10, *The Sixties Revolution and the Fall of Social Credit*.

4   Jamie Wilson and Allyson Quince's book *City of Champions* provides broad coverage of the various sports teams and programs in Edmonton, as well as details on some of the key players on these teams.

GROWTH, IMMIGRATION, AND PROSPERITY

1   John Gilpin provides an illuminating history of many of Edmonton's key movers and shakers, describing the individuals and their business enterprises. *Edmonton: Gateway to the North* is a worthy read.

2   Fil Fraser's *Alberta's Camelot* provides an in-depth and personal summary of culture and the arts during the Premier Lougheed years.

3   A lively account of the era may be found in Paul Bunner (ed.), *Alberta in the Twentieth Century (Vol. 11): Lougheed and the War with Ottawa*.

4   Details about league activities can be found in the specific historic files held by each league and at the EFCL office. Some have been archived at the City of Edmonton archives. Additional information may also be gleaned from back issues of the *Edmonton Journal* and the *Edmonton Examiner*.

5   Further details about the area councils are available through each council's chair, and through the EFCL office or website. Also refer to Appendix 2 "About Area Councils."

6   More details regarding the background to Policy C110, which recognizes the leagues as formal representatives of their community, may be found in the EFCL January 1980 report titled *Report from the City/Federation Relationship Committee*.

PICKING UP THE SLACK, AGAIN

1   An easy-to-read and extensive coverage of the economic and political conditions in the 1980s and the 1990s may be found in Volume 12, *Alberta Takes the Lead*, of Bunner's *Alberta in the Twentieth Century* series.

2   Jamie Wilson and Allyson Quince provide a great coverage of the era in the context of Edmonton. Their book *Edmonton: City of Champions* describes the many facets of life in the city, from living here to sports and festivals, to arts, leisure and business. A good read. Also interesting but a little dated is Kate Hildebrandt's summary of the 1980s in the book *Edmonton: The New Best West*.

3   The City of Edmonton planning department has a number of documents on the state of affairs in the city. These can be easily found through a basic search at any of the Edmonton Public Library facilities. One such publication, *Edmonton Profile 1997*, provides many valuable statistics.

4   A summary of Edmonton's festivals is available in *Edmonton: City of Festivals* by J. Parker, as well as in *City of Champions* by Jamie Wilson and Allyson Quince.

5   The EFCL holds in its office a number of interesting reports about its revitalization process, which could be extremely instructive to organizations that are looking at ways to get back on track amidst dysfunctional activity at board level. Valuable readings among these are the Leonard Apedaile report *Grassroots Community Leaders Speak Out: Results of the 1998 Community League Survey*, the 1998 Revitalization Task Force's *Preliminary Report*, and the 2000 Revitalization Implementation Team's final report titled *Foundation for the Future*.

REINVENTING AND REINVESTING

1   A valuable resource on the Revitalization Implementation Team's recommendations is its 2000 final report titled *Foundation For The Future*.

2   For a history of playgrounds in Edmonton and an analysis of their current status, please see the EFCL report *Teetering and Tottering: Playgrounds in Edmonton*, written by Chelsey Knievel and produced by the federation in 2002.

Bibliography

Alberta Public Safety Services. 1991. *Tornado, a report: Edmonton and Strathcona County July 31st 1987.* Edmonton: APSS.

Berton, P. 1967. *Klondike: The life and death of the last great gold rush.* Toronto: McClelland and Stewart.

———. 1978. *The wild frontiers: More tales from the remarkable past.* Toronto: McClelland and Stewart.

———. 1984. *The promised land: Settling the West 1896–1914.* Toronto: McClelland and Stewart.

———. 2001. *Marching as to war: Canada's turbulent years 1899–1953.* Toronto: Random House.

Bowler, V., and M. Wanchuk. 1986. *Volunteers: A history of the largest volunteer organization in North America.* Edmonton: Lone Pine.

Broadfoot, B. 1973. *Ten lost years: 1929–1939.* Toronto: Doubleday Canada.

Brown, C. R., and R. Cook. 1974. *Canada 1896–1921: A nation transformed.* Toronto: McClelland and Stewart.

Bunner, P., ed. 2003. *Alberta in the twentieth century.* 12 vols. Edmonton: History Books Publications.

Cashman, T. 1979. *Edmonton Exhibition: The first hundred years.* Edmonton: Edmonton Exhibition Association.

———. 2002. *Edmonton: Stories from the river city.* Edmonton: University of Alberta Press.

Chalmer, J. W., ed. 1985. *Looking back: King Edward Park and district.* Edmonton: Book Committee, King Edward Park Community League.

Commonwealth Historic Resource Management. 2004. *Rossdale Historical Land Use Study.* Vancouver: CHRM.

Creighton, D. 1976. *The Forked Road: Canada 1939–1957.* Toronto: McClelland and Stewart.

Edmonton Bulletin. Various articles.

Edmonton Journal. Various articles.

Edmonton Planning and Development. 1997. *Edmonton Profile 1997.* Edmonton: City of Edmonton.

Edmonton Federation of Community Leagues. January 1977. *The relationship between the city of Edmonton's community leagues and the Corporation of the City of Edmonton.* Edmonton: EFCL.

———. January 1980. *Report from the city/federation relations committee.* Edmonton: EFCL.

———. 1996. *Continued community commitment: EFCL 1921–1996.* Edmonton: R. Sheps and Associates.

———. January 2002. *A memory box: A play by Mary-Ellen Perley.* Unpublished script.

———. August 2002. *Teetering and Tottering: Playgrounds in Edmonton.* Edmonton: EFCL.

———. November 2002. *Evolution of the EFCL district structure: A history of area councils.* Edmonton: EFCL.

———. 2003. *EFCL business plan 2004–2006.* (Unpublished report.) Edmonton: EFCL.

Edmonton Federation of Community Leagues, Revitalization Implementation Team. January 2000. *Mandate and structure recommendations: Preliminary discussion paper.* Edmonton: EFCL.

———. March, 2000. *Foundation for change.* Edmonton: EFCL.

Edmonton Federation of Community Leagues, Revitalization Task Force. June 1998. *Preliminary report on the EFCL.* Edmonton: EFCL.

Fraser, F. 2003. *Alberta's Camelot: Culture and the arts in the Lougheed years.* Edmonton: Lone Pine.

Gilpin, John F. 1984. *Edmonton: Gateway to the North.* Edmonton: Windsor Publications.

Haggart R., and A. E. Golden. 1971. *Rumours of war.* Toronto: New Press.

Hesketh, B., and F. Swyripa, eds. 1995. *Edmonton: The life of a city.* Edmonton: NeWest Press.

Herzog, L. 2002. *The life of a neighbourhood: A history of Edmonton's Oliver district, 1870 to 1950.* Edmonton: Oliver Community League.

———. 2002. *Built on coal: A history of Beverly, Edmonton's working-class town.* Edmonton: Beverly Community Development Society.

Hildebrandt, K. 1991. *Edmonton, the new best west: A contemporary portrait.* Burlington, ON: Windsor Publications.

MacGregor, J. G. 1975. *Edmonton: A history.* 2nd ed. Edmonton: Hurtig Publishers.

Mair, A. 2000. *Gateway city: Stories from Edmonton's past.* Calgary: Fifth House.

Morton, W. L. 1963. *The kingdom of Canada: A general history from earlier times.* Toronto: McClelland and Stewart.

Newman, P. C. 1985. *Company of adventurers.* Markham, ON: Penguin.

Nicholson, G. W. L. 1964. *Canadian expeditionary force 1914–1919: Official history of the Canadian army in the First World War.* Ottawa: Queen's Printers.

Parker, J. 2002. *Edmonton: City of festivals.* Calgary: Weigl Educational Publishers.

Person, D., and C. Routledge. 1981. *Edmonton: Portrait of a city.* Edmonton: Reidmore Books.

Peters, Thomas J. 1994. *The Tom Peters seminar: Crazy times call for crazy organizations.* New York: Vintage.

Rooke, C. 2001. *Edmonton: Secrets of the city.* Vancouver: Arsenal Pulp Press.

Rogers, E. 1975. *History made in Edmonton.* Edmonton: Douglas Printing.

Shute, A., and M. Fortier. 1992. *Riverdale: From Fraser Flats to Edmonton oasis.* Edmonton: Tree Frog Press.

South Edmonton Papaschase Historical Society. 1984. *South Edmonton Saga.* Edmonton: SEPHS.

Stacey, C. P. 1948. *The Canadian army 1939–1945: An official historical summary.* Ottawa: Queen's Printers.

———. (1955). *Six years of war: The army in Canada, Britain and the Pacific.* Ottawa: Queen's Printers.

Stanley, G. F. G. 1974. *Canada's soldiers: The military history of an unmilitary people.* 3rd ed. Toronto: Macmillan.

Tingley, K. 1990. *The Strathcona dream: A photographic impression 1891–1920.* Edmonton: Old Strathcona Foundation.

Walters, M. 2002. *CKUA: Radio worth fighting for.* Edmonton: University of Alberta Press.

Wilson, J., and A. Quince. 1999. *City of champions.* Edmonton: City of Champions. Yanish, L., and S. Lowe. 1991. *Edmonton's west side story.* Edmonton: 124th Street and Area Business Association.

Index

Bold page numbers refer to photographs.

About the Author

R ON KUBAN HAS EXTENSIVE EXPERIENCE with Edmonton's community league movement. For over twenty years, he has served in many capacities including his local community league, the area council, and the Edmonton Federation of Community Leagues (EFCL). At the league level, Ron served in various Board positions and was involved in diverse projects from community beautification to playground and park development. As a member, and later chair of the Mill Woods Presidents' Council, he also co-chaired three of the council's Canada Day celebrations, which in 2004 attracted more than 45,000 visitors. From 1999 to 2002, he served as president of the EFCL during its revitalization.

Ron Kuban has volunteered for many community-based organizations including the Mill Woods Community Patrol (founding member), the Mill Woods Soccer Association (board member, coach), and the Edmonton Regional Crime Prevention Network Society (founding chair).

Ron Kuban graduated with a BA from the Royal Military College of Canada as well as an MEd and a PhD from the University of Alberta. In 2003, he received the Queen's Jubilee medal for his community service.